Folk Songs from the West Virginia Hills

SOUNDING APPALACHIA
Travis D. Stimeling, Series Editor

TITLES IN THE SERIES
_____

Fifty Cents and a Box Top:
The Creative Life of Nashville Session Musician Charlie McCoy
Charlie McCoy with Travis D. Stimeling

PATRICK W. GAINER
1903 - 1981

FOLK SONGS FROM THE WEST VIRGINIA HILLS

Foreword by

EMILY HILLIARD

WEST VIRGINIA UNIVERSITY PRESS
MORGANTOWN • 2017

First edition published 1975
by Seneca Books
Second edition published 2017
by West Virginia University Press

ISBN:
PB: 978-1-946684-03-5

Cover design by Than Saffel. Cover photograph courtesy
of the West Virginia and Regional History Collection,
West Virginia University Libraries.

To Toni

CONTENTS

xi

FOREWORD

When I first interviewed 89-year-old ballad singer Phyllis Marks at her Gilmer County home, I asked her how she started performing her songs and stories. She told me about the first time she met Dr. Patrick Gainer, when he was looking for local performers for the first West Virginia State Folk Festival:

"Well when I was at school, I would say great long poems but I didn't sing in public. And Dr. Patrick Gainer went to Webster County to see my mother but she wouldn't come down. And I was living on Lynch Run so they come up there on Lynch Run to see if I knew the songs . . . any old songs, and I did—I sang some. I was kinda bashful. And he said, 'well your voice is not very loud but there'll be a microphone there.' And I said, 'See all these kids, I can't sing without a rocking chair!' And when I went to the stage there was a rocking chair! I didn't really mean it."[1]

Marks laughed remembering how she ribbed Dr. Gainer. Though the two are from the same county, I imagine a perceived power imbalance between them, at least in that initial encounter. Dr. Gainer, the esteemed professor from the public university, was the one holding the microphone, with the authority to put Marks on a stage. Her joke was a playful disruption of that hierarchy. After her initial performance, Phyllis became an active performer and recognized tradition bearer in her Gilmer County community and beyond, recording for the Library of Congress and performing concerts across the greater Appalachian region including all but one of the West Virginia State Folk Festivals in Glenville since Gainer founded it in 1950. (She missed the 2015 event due to illness.) According to folklorist Gerry Milnes, Marks is today the last active ballad singer in the state who learned the song tradition completely through oral transmission from her family members. Phyllis has always sung traditional ballads, but her artistry and knowledge is her own. While I don't put too much import on the notion of "discovery" by folklorists, it is on account of her ethnographic relationship with Patrick Gainer that we know of Phyllis Marks today.

I never met Patrick Gainer—he died before I was born and long before I set foot in West Virginia. But nearly forty years after his death, I still feel the effects of his influence on the preservation and support of the traditional culture of West Virginia and the people who practice it. Stories like Phyllis's provide a firsthand account of his character, affirming what I have read in his biographies and deduce from his own writing. While he was an esteemed professor, he was also a West Virginia native who grew up in the singing tradition. He approached the people he collected songs from as his peers and brethren, a regrettably rare perspective among folk song collectors of his era. His ability to shoot from both hips—as the musicologist scholar and as the insider from a family of ballad singers—is evident in all his work. When he set out the rocking chair on the stage for Phyllis, I like to think he did so both out of respect for her as an equal, and with a wink and a nod—obeying her request in a willing shift of power . . . and maybe just a little insecurity as to whether she really meant it.

Patrick Gainer was born in Parkersburg in 1903 (some sources say 1904) to a musical family of Irish descent. He was raised on a farm in the village of Tanner in Gilmer County in the central part of the state. His home county became the locus of his song collecting activity, an endeavor he began at age twenty-one when he was a student at West Virginia University. Working with faculty member Carey Woofter, the two formed a song collecting duo sans recording technology, with Woofter transcribing the words and Gainer notating the melody. Some of the songs from those collecting excursions are included in this volume, while the others—collected after 1950—were recorded on tape and transcribed later. The remainder, as Gainer notes in his introduction, were imprinted in his mind as a child via the singing of his grandfather Francis C. Gainer: "These songs lived in my own memory just as they had lived in the memory of my ancestors." The majority of the songs included in *Folk Songs from the West Virginia Hills* were collected in Gilmer County, with fourteen total counties represented, mostly in the central part of the state.

At WVU, Gainer studied under John Harrington Cox, a Harvard-trained folklorist who published the first extensive state-focused collection of folk songs, *Folk Songs of the South*.[2] In 1926 Gainer married Antoinette Kizinski, an immigrant from Poland. Together they raised five children.[3]

After receiving his bachelor's and master's degrees from WVU, Gainer took an English professor position at St. Louis University, where he also employed his warbly tenor as director of the Glee Club. While in St. Louis, he began work on his dissertation, studying with University of Chicago folklorist Archer Taylor.[4] Gainer earned his PhD in 1933 and remained in St. Louis until 1942 when he moved to New York to become director of training for the United Service Organization during WWII.

After the war, Dr. Gainer returned to West Virginia, upon accepting an English professor position at his alma mater, West Virginia University. During that academic era, folklore courses were generally embedded in English departments; Gainer taught classes in folklore of the southern Appalachians, as well as in Milton and nineteenth-century literature.[5] A beloved teacher, his courses were "among the most popular offered at the institution."[6] Gainer estimated that he taught over 12,000 students at the university, encouraging many to explore and document their own family's cultural heritage.[7] In 1950, he founded the West Virginia Folk Festival in Glenville, the county seat of his home county. He directed the festival for ten years and was a frequent performer, singing ballads accompanied by a rebec, the instrument he believed to be the forerunner of the mountain dulcimer. During his tenure at WVU, Gainer published the *West Virginia Centennial Book of 100 Songs, 1863–1963* (1963) and recorded the album *Folk Songs of the Allegheny Mountains* for Folk Heritage Recordings (1963).[8, 9] In the years after his 1972 retirement, Gainer contributed the "Music" chapter to B. B. Maurer's *Mountain Heritage* (1974) and published two books, *Witches, Ghosts, and Signs* (1975) and *Folk Songs from the West Virginia Hills* (1975).[10, 11, 12] Patrick Gainer died on February 22, 1981, at age 77. He is buried at Good Shepherd Cemetery in his hometown of Tanner.

Gainer's annotations in *Folk Songs from the West Virginia Hills* show his intimate relationship with the oral mountain song tradition. For the sometimes acerbic Gainer, his passion was both a source of personal pride and a root of cynicism. "Most people wish to be entertained by professional entertainers and not by parents and grandparents singing old songs in the home. What young person would turn off the latest popular program on the television tube to hear Grandma sing 'Lord Bateman?'" he implores. Still, Gainer is not a purist; he acknowledges that change is an inherent element of the evolution and persistence of traditional culture. In his introduction to *Folk Songs*, he notes that some popular songs, like those of Stephen Foster, can pass into oral tradition, and his song headnotes, particularly for the Child Ballads, are rife with examples of the evolution of folk songs—how titles change respective of location, themes are altered according to community values, and verses are lost or gained. In his essay "Tradition" in the foundational collection *Eight Words for the Study of Expressive Culture,* folklorist Henry Glassie expounds on this inevitable progression: "But tradition is the opposite of only one kind of change: that in which disruption is so complete that the new cannot be read as an innovative adaptation of the old."[13] Gainer seems to believe that recorded music, radio, television, and written music constitute just such a disruption of the orally transmitted mountain song tradition. The irony, perhaps, of his view of written and recorded music as oppressive forces that turn the masses into consumers rather than participants in their own culture, is that the book that follows is, effectively, written music. But it is clear that his presentation of these collected songs is intended not only as a product of his own work, but evidence of the creative contribution and talent of his own mountaineers. Gainer's motivation is to preserve and validate that tradition through text.

In the second half of his introduction, Gainer relates a brief history of West Virginians and a deconstruction of the "hillbilly" stereotype to which he takes offense. He offers a counter narrative of mountaineers as hardworking, skilled, religious people, who are deeply rooted in the oral tradition of their Irish, Scottish, English, and German ancestors. It should be noted that Gainer is speaking of his own family and community here; he does not mention other races or ethnicities outside of those from these four European countries. It's unfortunate that the documentation of music from other immigrant and cultural communities—the Italians, Poles, Hungarians, Greeks, and others, as well as African Americans who moved to West Virginia from the deep south to work in the coal mines and other industries—was not common among folk song collectors of this era; I regret what was never documented and hence, lost. While Gainer does present a personal profile of the Scots-Irish music tradition during his lifetime, other ethnicities are generally excluded from his scope, which he nonetheless posits as being an authoritative depiction of West Virginia's traditional music.

Like his mentor Cox in his collection *Folk Songs of the South* fifty years prior, Gainer gives preference to the Scottish and English ballads, known as Child Ballads, that were cataloged by American folklore scholar Francis James Child in the late 1800s. Child published these 305 traditional ballads and their variants in the ten-volume *English and Scottish Popular Ballads,* with the final edition appearing in 1898.[14] Though Child collected these songs via epistolary research and concerned himself only with text, never having heard the melodies from the traditional singers themselves, and despite the guidelines for his curatorial decisions being somewhat obtuse, his numbered collection remains a touchstone today.[15] Most Child Ballads can be traced back to the seventeenth and eighteenth centuries, though a few, Gainer says, date as far back as the thirteenth century. Gainer reports collecting fifty of the 305 in West Virginia, adding to Cox's previously documented thirty-four. Gainer lists each of the fifty in the numerical order of the original Child catalog numbers but gives preference to the West Virginia title of the song over Child's title. Often these West Virginia variants feature local place names, as in "Child 2, The Elfin Knight," which

Gainer collected from Moses Ayres of Calhoun County, who called it "O Where Are You Going? I'm Going to Linn." In one case, with the song "John Randal," known as "Lord Randall" in Child's collection, Gainer's consultant, Mr. W. A. Thomas of Erbacon in Webster County, claimed he knew the Randal family who, according to him, lived just across the mountain.[16] In Gainer's "Music" chapter in Maurer's *Mountain Heritage*, Gainer recalls this recording excursion and acknowledges the adaptation of narrative to a local story, even though the original version dates to seventeenth-century Italy.[17] Rather than dispute or correct his consultant, Gainer accepts both of these truths, commenting, "Of course I did not tell him that the ballad could not have been made up about the poisoning of John Randal who lived over the mountain, for I was the one who came to learn from him. This adaptation of an old-world ballad to an incident which took place in America is unusual, but it does sometimes occur."[18, 19]

In the headnotes of several Child Ballads, Gainer implies that variations in song texts display the moral and religious values of the community in which they are found. In the West Virginia version of the "Elfin Knight," the title character has lost the supernatural status of the original narrative, and is portrayed instead as a young mortal teasing his former beloved. Gainer writes, "The preternatural world of fairies and elves does not survive in the folklore of West Virginia because of the strong puritanical influence. The fairies generally were a benevolent folk who helped man, but since good could come only from God, and fairies were not in the Bible, they could not exist." He also attributes the persistence of those ballads with tragic themes to their moral lesson, and the decline of others, like Child 299, "The Soldier and the Maid," because they were not suitable for children and, hence, weren't sung in mountain homes. I'm struck by how many of the Child Ballads that Gainer collected in West Virginia are centered around strong female characters who have agency over their own lives. These themes are still in the minority, but many—like "The Six King's Daughters" in which the principle character throws her suitor in the sea, or "The Devil's Questions" in which a maid outsmarts the devil's riddles—depict empowered women. If ballads had a Bechdel test, I'd posit at least a half dozen would pass.[20]

While Gainer's headnotes to each song throughout the collection rely on his dual status as academic expert and member of the source community, his tone is accessible and genial rather than analytical and incisive. Though he does include a brief, final section of his introduction explaining the modes, scales, and musicological structures of the folk songs that follow, his intended audience favors the general public over academic scholars, and for this he has been criticized within the academy. In the 1977 issue of the *Appalachian Journal*, scholar David Whisnat calls the collection "too superficial to be of much use."[21] It is admittedly curious that Gainer chose the transcription method of song collecting at a time when his colleagues were using recording technology; WVU folklorist Louis W. Chappell, whom Gainer accompanied on recording trips, had been doing field recordings since at least 1937.[22] Perhaps as an undergraduate or master's student, Gainer did not have the necessary funding for equipment. I regret that we do not have recordings of the examples in this collection, though Gainer's chosen media is additional evidence of his intended audience; a book, particularly one that is constructed as a songbook, is much more accessible to the general public than a collection of field recordings sitting in a university archive. Additionally, Gainer's presentation of the songs in this collection mirrors his approach as a fieldworker—he gives enough information to provide context in a pithy narrative and then gets out of the way so the singer can sing her song.

In the second section, "Other Ballads and Folk Songs," Gainer presents thirty-two songs, of which he says eighteen are ballads. It is unclear, however, what he considers a ballad as opposed to a folk song. In the headnotes to the individual songs, he only calls five of them ballads—a sixth, "The Drummer of Waterloo," he identifies in the introduction as the only ballad of the eighteen that is completely of old world origin. And he refers to "One Morning in May" as both a song and a ballad. His categorization does not appear to be related to whether the selection was originally printed as a broadside, nor whether its origin is the British Isles, West Virginia, or parts unknown. Essentially, this chapter functions as a catchall category for those songs (or ballads) that were not cataloged by Child, and are not sung fiddle tunes, nor of a religious nature. These songs and ballads convey a range of emotions—from tragedy to humor to heroics. Of particular note are two West Virginia native songs, "John Henry" and "John Hardy." Though Gainer's mentor John Harrington Cox lists them as the same song in his 1925 collection, fifty years later it had been established by folk song scholars that they are clearly two separate songs, both in text and melody. While both narratives are set in West Virginia and feature African American men with similar names, that is the extent of their commonality. "John Henry," the labor story of the working man, likely a former slave, who bests the industrial machine but dies doing so, is one of the most renowned folk songs and folk allegories in the entire history of American music. "John Hardy," however, tells the much smaller story of a "bad, bad man" (in some versions a "desperate little man") who shoots a man during a game of cards at a coal camp in McDowell County.

"Fiddle-Tune Songs" features seven fiddle tunes with sung words, like "Shady Grove," "Sourwood Mountain," and "Old Joe Clark." All but one are well-known and not exclusive to West Virginia. "Paper of Pins," the oddball in the group, is known more as a play party song than a fiddle tune. The song is part of Phyllis Marks' active repertoire; she recently sang it at a West Virginia Folklife concert at the Humanities Council in Charleston.[23] It is here that Gainer asserts his claim that the mountain dulcimer, or as he calls it, the "plucked dulcimer," is a descendant of the Arabic rebec, which he says came to America from the British Isles but was overshadowed by the fiddle. Gainer, who shared this theory with John Jacob Niles of Kentucky, was steadfast in this opinion, asserting in the 1968 *Nicholas County News Leader*, ". . . what we think of as the dulcimer today is not sailing under its true name." In Gerry Milnes's 1999 book *Play of a Fiddle* on the traditional music of West Virginia, Milnes explores Gainer's claim, noting that dulcimers were often referred to as "zithers," suggesting the instrument's German origins.[24]

The fourth and fifth chapters of the book are both composed of religious songs, but are separated by race, entitled respectively, "Choral Singing in the Mountains" and "The Negro Contribution." As to this segregation and cringe-worthy title, some may defend Gainer as a product of his time, but I'm wary of the allowances that can follow when that excuse is entertained. In "Choral Singing in the Mountains" Gainer writes as an insider to his own community: "Even before *our* pioneer ancestors built their churches in the wilderness . . ." [emphasis my own]. However, in the following chapter, no such inclusive language is used, suggesting that Gainer does not consider African Americans to be part of his own folk group, nor assume them to be among his readers. In the headnote to the first of the six songs in this section, Gainer writes, "It should be noted that in printing the songs in this book, we have not used any dialectal pronunciations." He goes on to explain that "speech is not racial," but addressing this point in the last fifteen pages of the book in a chapter that already separates black music from white further emphasizes his exclusion of African Americans in his assumed audience and home community. This is problematic, perhaps most importantly because it portrays the black and white gospel, ballad, and folk song traditions as being historically more separate than they actually were. In fact, Appalachian music is at its core an amalgam of traditions, notably African American, Native American, and Anglo-Saxon, though regrettably, the African American and Native contributions have long been suppressed, denied, and ignored. In the song headnotes, Gainer writes that "these songs have been sung just as much by white Americans through the years," but that statement should be inverted; many of the songs in the other sections of the book were sung and played by black musicians and string bands, and due to the preference of folk song collectors for the Anglo-Saxon tradition, many other instances and songs of black musicians remain undocumented. Gainer does attest in the chapter's introduction that African Americans have made the greatest contribution to American folk music over any other ethnic group or race, but his approach here is nearsighted at best, racist and irresponsible at worst.

Books, like people, are imperfect, and cultural documentation is always filtered through the lens and curatorial choices of the collector. I address the flaws and triumphs of *Folk Songs from the West Virginia Hills* not to invalidate nor overinflate the work, but to understand and contextualize it; as readers we always carry the point of view of our own historical moment, for better or worse. In 2017, the 1975 *Folk Songs* not only tells us about the evolution of the mountain song tradition over forty years, but also the evolution of the *study* of mountain song tradition. We thankfully have become more inclusive and accurate in our understanding of Appalachian music as a blend of cultural traditions. While there's progress yet to be made, we have shed much of the racial separation and suppression that was present in folkloric study of Gainer's era.

Writing in 1975, Gainer considered there to be "almost no oral tradition in America today to preserve song in memory." Undoubtedly he saw changes that amounted to a decline in participation of his beloved mountain singing tradition, but over forty years later, that light is still shining. Phyllis Marks still performs with her granddaughter, swaps songs with her caregiver, and shares stories with collectors like me. Trevor Hammons, the fifteen-year-old great grandson of legendary banjo picker Lee Hammons, placed fifth in the adult category banjo contest at the Appalachian String Band Music Festival at Clifftop in 2016.[25] And though additional instruments and amplification might make it unrecognizable to Gainer, West Virginia's gospel tradition is continuous and ever vibrant, as evidenced by the Gospel Singaleers of Beckley and Mount Hope's Ethel Caffie-Austin, among others. While many mountaineers today may not learn "the old songs" through oral transmission the way Gainer and Marks did, Gainer has offered a road map that may spur a memory of a song that a grandparent used to sing, a sung fiddle tune that a neighbor plays, or a spiritual from a childhood church service. Additionally, new songs enter the folk tradition all the time. This collection exists as one of many examples of the rich cultural traditions that are embedded in daily life in West Virginia. And at a time when West Virginians are still combatting mainstream negative stereotypes all too similar to what Gainer experienced in 1975, documents like this are objects of resistance.

Folk Songs from the West Virginia Hills and other folkloric documentation can serve as a mirror to show us the culture we have, but also what we've lost and gained along the way, for better or for worse. Throughout the collection, Gainer provides evidence of how folk songs are distilled democratic cultural nuggets of a community, conveying the values of its people. He declares, "They are called folk songs because they belong to the people and not any one individual."[26] Folklorist Lynne McNeill says this another way: "Group consensus shapes folklore, so folklore is a great measure of group consensus." I, for one, am proud to live and work in a place where the group consensus is for singing.

NOTES

1. Marks, Phyllis. Interview by Emily Hilliard. April 2016.
2. John Harrington Cox, *Folk-Songs of the South*. Cambridge: Harvard University Press, 1925; Morgantown: West Virginia University Press, 2013.
3. Paul Gartner, "Dr. Gainer: Folk Festival Founder," *Goldenseal*, Volume 26, Number 2, Summer 2000, 58–59.
4. "Patrick Ward Gainer Child Ballads of West Virginia," West Virginia History Digital Collections, West Virginia and Regional History Collection, accessed May 1, 2017, https://lib.wvu.edu/collections/patrickgainer.
5. Gainer alludes to Milton's poem *L'Allegro* in the "Fiddle-Tune Songs" chapter of the book.
6. John H. Randolph, "Pat Gainer," in *The West Virginia Encyclopedia*, ed. Ken Sullivan. Charleston: The West Virginia Humanities Council, 2006.
7. Gerry Milnes. *Play of a Fiddle*. (Lexington: The University Press of Kentucky, 1999), 136.
8. Patrick Gainer. *West Virginia Centennial Book of 100 Songs, 1863–1963*. Morgantown: West Virginia University Press, 1963.
9. Patrick Gainer. *Folk Songs of the Allegheny Mountains*. Folk Heritage Recordings, 1963.
10. B. B. Maurer, ed., *Mountain Heritage*, Parsons: McClain Printing Company, 1974.
11. Patrick Gainer. *Witches, Ghosts, and Signs*. Morgantown: West Virginia University Press, 2008.
12. Patrick Gainer. *Folk Songs from the West Virginia Hills*. Grantsville: Seneca Books, 1975.
13. Henry Glassie, "Tradition," in *Eight Words for the Study of Expressive Culture*, ed. Burt Feintuch. (Urbana and Chicago: University of Illinois Press, 2003), 177.
14. Francis Child. *English and Scottish Popular Ballads*. Mineola: Dover Publications, 2003.
15. Rob Young. *Electric Eden: Unearthing Britain's Visionary Music*. (London: Faber and Faber, 2010), 68–69.
16. I was trained to use the term "consultant" for ethnographic inter-viewees/participants, as per Luke Eric Lassiter's *The Chicago Guide to Collaborative Ethnography*. Chicago: University of Chicago Press, 2005. This term implies an equal dynamic between folklorist/ethnographer and consultant, as they are both experts in their own field and experience.
17. Patrick Gainer, "Music" in *Mountain Heritage*, ed. B. B. Maurer. Parsons: McClain Printing Company, 1974.
18. Gainer, "Music," 147.
19. Gerry Milnes documents a similar instance in regards to the murder ballad "Omie Wise." Though the original story took place in North Carolina, as documented via court records and other documents, a community of

Milnes's consultants in Randolph County cite a similar story taking place in West Virginia. Milnes, *Play of a Fiddle*, 77–86.

20. In her 1985 comic strip, *Dykes to Watch Out For*, cartoonist Alison Bechdel presented the idea of what is now known as "The Bechdel Test" or "Bechdel-Wallace Test" for movies and other works of fiction to assess the presence and agency of female characters. The criteria are that there must be at least two women who talk to each other about something other than a man. Since Child Ballads often only have two characters, a version of the Bechdel test would likely have criteria including at least one woman with agency who speaks about something other than a man.

21. David Whisnat, *Appalachian Journal*.

22. Milnes, *Play of a Fiddle*, 7.

23. Phyllis Marks. *West Virginia Folklife Presents Phyllis Marks*. Live Concert. West Virginia Humanities Council, Charleston. September 8, 2016.

24. Milnes, *Play of a Fiddle*, 138.

25. Gainer collected songs from Hammons family member Maggie Hammons Parker, two of which are included in *Songs from the West Virginia Hills*.

26. Patrick Gainer, "Music" in *Mountain Heritage*, ed. B. B. Maurer. Parsons: McClain Printing Company, 1974.

INTRODUCTION

The songs in this volume have been collected in West Virginia over a period of fifty years, beginning in 1924. I wrote many of them down before the tape recorder came into use, from the singing of people who had preserved them in their family traditions for many generations. After 1950 most of the songs were recorded on tape recorders. But many of them had been recorded in my own mind when I was a small boy in the early part of this century, from the singing of my grandfather, Francis C. Gainer and others of his generation, so that these songs lived in my own memory just as they had lived in the memories of my ancestors.

With a few exceptions the songs are folk songs. Even the hymns whose composers are known, and which may be found in print just as they were written, passed into oral tradition and eventually became folk songs. A true folk song is a song that has been preserved in oral tradition for at least several generations. Folk songs are not the property of any individual but belong to all the people who wish to sing them. One cannot secure a copyright for the words and tune of a true folk song. One cannot compose a folk song, though he may write an imitation of one. Poets have composed narrative poems in the style of folk ballads, but these poems are not true folk ballads. For example, Dante Gabriel Rosetti wrote many narrative poems in the style of the old folk ballads, such as "Sister Helen." Today there are many popular singers who sing songs they themselves have composed which they call folk songs, but these are merely songs which become popular for a short time and never become traditional.

It is possible that one might write a song which would pass into oral tradition and in time become a folk song, as happened with some of Stephen Foster's songs. However, this is not likely to happen to modern popular song, for there is almost no oral tradition in America today to preserve song in memory; everything that is needed in song is provided by records, radio, television, and written music.

In recent years many churches have accepted popular music in their religious services because it has an appeal to a large number of people who have been oriented by radio and television. This singing usually is accompanied by guitar music, for it is the mistaken belief that folk singing is always accompanied by guitar or other string instrument— which has never been true in America.

We are now living in "an age which has an outrageous thirst for gross and violent stimulant." Most people wish to be entertained by professional entertainers and not by parents and grandparents singing old songs in the home. What young person would turn off the latest popular program on the television tube to hear Grandma sing "Lord Bateman?" Or what housewife would desert her favorite soap opera to sing "Billy Boy" to the children?

Most of us have become silent listeners of the music which comes to us from outside the home, instead of being participants in singing, story telling, and playing traditional games within the home. Thus we have little oral traditions.

This vast change in home life came about gradually in the days following World War I, when the radio became the center of family life, especially in the evening hours. Family singing began to decline. The singing school and the weekly singing at the church soon ceased. Communities which had long been known for their good singers now had difficulty in forming a choir even for a funeral service. Today most funeral homes use recordings of music over loudspeaker systems.

Since the songs in this book have been sung to me by many people in their homes among the hills of West Virginia, I feel that I should tell something about these people whose ancestors chose as the motto of their state, *Montani Semper Liberi,* "Mountaineers Always Free." There is a widespread belief among people whose knowledge of the mountain people has been gained from fiction, pictures and stories in the press, and programs on radio and television, that the part of the United States called "Appalachia" is a region of poverty, depression, loneliness, and ignorance, whose inhabitants are called "hillbillies." The West Virginia "hillbilly" is pictured as a kind of degenerate character whose chief occupation is making moonshine; he goes without shoes, wears dirty, ragged clothes, a ragged hat with a pointed crown, and is usually found asleep near his still or sitting on the porch of his little shack while his woman does the work. To true West Virginia mountaineers the term "hillbilly" is highly derogatory. It is as insulting to us as such terms as "nigger," "hunkie," "kike," and "wop" are to other people.

The people who first came into this region were mostly of Irish, Scottish, English, and German ancestry. The ancestors of many of us came to America in the early part of the eighteenth century, and many of them fought in the Revolutionary War. Many German people came into the Shenandoah Valley from Pennsylvania and later moved west over the Alleghenies. Many of the Irish and Scotch came into Maryland, then moved south and west into the mountains. Many of the English came into Virginia, thence west over the mountains.

These people were farmers. They moved west into the Allegheny Mountains and the valleys of the foothills, extending west to the Ohio valley, because there was much land to be bought at low prices, and they sought freedom from the oppression of rich land owners which they had experienced in their old-world environment. They came to the hill country, where they found rich bottom lands for grain fields, and meadows and fertile hillsides that could be turned into bluegrass pasture.

They could bring with them only the most necessary things for living, but they knew how to build houses and furnish them with home-made furniture. They knew how to grow flax to be made into linen clothing, and they could spin and weave the wool from the sheep which they raised. They brought few books besides the Bible, but in their minds they carried a great store of traditional knowledge, and in their hearts a love for the best that had been told in story and song by their ancestors for countless generations. Even the language they used was largely that which had been preserved in oral tradition. Some of the words they used had not changed from the time of Chaucer. The word "ferninst" in "Will The Weaver" is pure Chaucerian. It means "opposite."

These pioneers were religious people. Even before they could build churches they cleared out patches of woods for meeting places, leaving stumps of trees for seats. Gradually villages formed, and these became centers where people came to buy items which could not be produced on the land, such as coffee and salt. Typical of these centers was the village of Tanner, near which I grew up. At the beginning of this century it had a hotel, two general stores, a hardware store, a barber shop, two blacksmith shops, a medical doctor with a good office, two churches, a large flour mill, a school, and a good brass band, with a bandwagon on which they traveled to other communities. The singing teachers came once or twice a year and taught the people to read music so they could sing the old hymns in harmony. There was a monthly gathering at the schoolhouse, called a "literary", which brought people in for miles. In harvest time people gathered at each other's homes to help with the work of stringing beans, peeling apples, shucking corn, or making molasses. These were great social gatherings also.

These people did not have much in the way of cash money, nor did they need much. Most of the buying of necessities at the store was done by barter. Eggs, chickens, rabbits, ginseng, hides and other products were traded for store goods.

Singing was a part of the daily lives of the family. As mother worked at canning or other household chores, she sang. As grandmother sat at her spinning wheel, she sang the songs she had learned as a girl and had kept "in her heart" through the years. On long winter evenings there was time after supper to gather before the fireplace to sing and tell stories. If a stranger came by, he was welcome to stay the night and to sit at the board with the family. There are many people today who think that the mountain people are suspicious of "outsiders" and receive them with hostility. I have traveled over the hills and hollows for a half century, recording folklore and encouraging people to be proud of their folk heritage, and never have I encountered any sign of hostility, but always a genuine show of friendliness.

The Musical Structure of Folk Songs

Many of the tunes in this book may sound strange to the modern listener. A young lady once told me: "Granny used to sing a lot, but I didn't think she could carry a tune very well, because she hardly ever ended a song on *Do.*" A brief explanation of the musical structure of folk songs will be helpful.

Our modern major scale is a musical structure of seven tones, with five whole-tone intervals and two half-tone intervals. Between the third and fourth tones and between the seventh and eighth tones are half-tone intervals; the rest are whole-tone intervals. Most songs with which the modern listener is familiar use this structure, the first tone of the scale being the "tonic" or "keynote," on which the song usually ends.

However, many of the folk tunes use an ancient system of "modes", in which the tone relations in the structure are not the same as in the modern major scale. These modes are ordinarily identified by their ancient Greek names: Ionian, Dorian, Phrygian, Lydian, Mixolydian, Aeolian, and Locrian. The modes most often used in the songs in the Allegheny Mountains are Mixolydian, Dorian, and Aeolian. Examples of songs in the Mixolydian mode: "The Devil's Questions" and "The Six King's Daughters." Examples of the Dorian mode are "Lord Bateman" and "What Wondrous Love." Examples of the Aeolian mode are "The Seven Sons" and "The Three Little Babes."

Another characteristic of many of the tunes is their use of the pentatonic, or five-tone, scale, in which there are only five tones with no half-tone intervals. This is often called the "gapped scale." The pentatonic tunes can be played on the black keys of the piano or organ. Examples of this scale are the tunes of "The Sister's Murder," "The Cherry Tree," and "The Riddle Song."

Accidentals almost never occur in the old-world tunes or in their American survivals. The flatted third does not occur in the old-world songs of white people, but it is almost always found in the "blues" song, a form originating with black singers. The same is true of the flatted seventh. Folk songs that were preserved in the traditions of home life were almost never accompanied by any kind of instrument, but those sung by minstrels or "county-fair singers" were always sung with accompaniment.

We have used the term "broadside" to describe the texts of some of the songs in this book. A broadside was originally a song printed on one side of a sheet of paper and sold in the streets. Later it came to mean any song that was distributed in printed form. These were often composed by "hack writers" and printed in books. In America such books as *The Forget-Me-Not Songster* were often carried into rural areas by itinerant peddlars. Songs that were first learned from this kind of book sometimes passed into oral tradition to become popular folk songs.

PART ONE
The Child Ballads

Fifty of the ballads in this volume have double titles. The first title is the one which the West Virginia singer used for the song. Below the first title, in parentheses, is the Child number, and in quotation marks is the title of the ballad as it appears in the work of Francis James Child, whose monumental work, *The English and Scottish Popular Ballads*, was published from 1882 to 1898, in ten parts, later combined into five volumes. Professor Child, a great Harvard scholar, made a detailed study of all the ballads which had been, or were currently, a part of English and Scottish tradition. He did not collect ballads directly from the people, but used the printed and manuscript collections that had been made in England and Scotland and in other countries of the world. Child traced the history and the origin of each ballad and its relation to the folk ballads of other countries. In his entire work he included 305 different ballads, with all the extant versions of each ballad. Some of the songs have been traced back to the thirteenth century; the same songs have been found in West Virginia with the words and the musical structure virtually unchanged. When a ballad is found in America which is a version of one of the ballads in the Child work, it is identified as Child, with its proper number in the Child work.

Dr. John Harrington Cox in *Folk Songs of the South*, 1925, reported thirty-four Child ballads found in West Virginia. Since then I have found a total of fifty Child ballads, with several versions of some of

1

them. For this volume I have selected only one version of each of these fifty Child ballads. The student of folklore should read Child's introductory notes to each of the Child ballads which we have found. Child's work has been reprinted in an inexpensive five-volume edition by Dover Publications.

THE DEVIL'S QUESTIONS

(CHILD 1, "RIDDLES WISELY EXPOUNDED")

This ballad has not been reported previously from West Virginia tradition. It was sung by Blanche Kelley, Gilmer County. The devil asks the maid difficult questions, which she must answer satisfactorily or be carried off to hell. When she answers the questions wisely, the devil disappears.

The word "peart" in the refrain is a dialect word meaning cheerful and becoming.

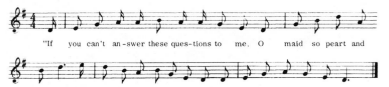

"If you can't an-swer these ques-tions to me, O maid so peart and bon - nie, Then you'll be mine and go·with me, And you so peart and bon - nie.

2 "O what is higher than the tree?
O maid so peart and bonnie,
And what is deeper than the sea?
And you so peart and bonnie.

3 "O what is louder than the horn?
O maid so peart and bonnie,
And what is earlier than the morn?
And you so peart and bonnie."

4 "O heaven is higher than the tree,
As I am peart and bonnie,
And hell is deeper than the sea,
And I am peart and bonnie.

5 "O thunder is louder than the horn,
As I am peart and bonnie,
And sin is earlier than the morn,
And I am peart and bonnie."

O WHERE ARE YOU GOING? I'M GOING TO LINN

(CHILD 2, "THE ELFIN KNIGHT")

In the old-world ballad of Child's work, the title of this ballad is "The Elfin Knight", but in the West Virginia versions the knight loses the character of the supernatural and is simply a young man who has a playful sort of game between himself and his former lover. He imposes certain impossible tasks upon her, and she in turn imposes even more impossible tasks upon him.

The preternatural world of fairies and elves does not survive in the folklore of West Virginia because of the strong puritanical influence. The fairies generally were a benevolent folk who helped man, but since good could come only from God, and fairies were not in the Bible, they could not exist. Therefore, the old-world ballads and stories of fairies did not survive in oral tradition, or were adapted to include only mortals. Sung by Moses Ayers, Calhoun County.

"O where are you go-ing?" "I'm go-ing to Linn." Fol-low ma la cus lone-lee. "Give my re-spects to a la-dy there-in." Ma kee ta lo. kee ta lo, tam-pa-lo, tam-pa-lo, Fol-low ma la cus lone-lee.

2 "I want her to make me a cambric shirt,"
    Follow ma la cus lonelee,
  "Without any thread or needle work,"
    Ma kee ta lo, kee ta lo, tam-pa-lo, tam-pa-lo,
    Follow ma la cus lonelee.

4

3 "I want her to wash it in yonder hill,"
       Follow ma la cus lonelee,
    "Where dew never was nor rain never fell,"
       Ma kee ta lo, kee ta lo, tam-pa-lo, tam-pa-lo,
       Follow ma la cus lonelee.

4 "I want her to dry it on yonder bush,"
       Follow ma la cus lonelee,
    "Where tree never bloomed since Adam was born,"
       Ma kee ta lo, kee ta lo, tam-pa-lo, tam-pa-lo,
       Follow ma la cus lonelee."

5 "Now since you have asked these questions of me,"
       Follow ma la cus lonelee,
    "And now I will ask as man of thee,"
       Ma kee ta lo, kee ta lo, tam-pa-lo, tam-pa-lo,
       Follow ma la cus lonelee.

6 "I want you to buy me an acre of land,"
       Follow ma la cus lonelee,
    "Between the salt sea and the salt land,"
       Ma kee ta lo, kee ta lo, tam-pa-lo, tam-pa-lo,
       Follow ma la cus lonelee.

7 "I want you to plow it with an old ox's horn,"
       Follow ma la cus lonelee,
    "And plant it all over with one kernel of corn,"
       Ma kee ta lo, kee ta lo, tam-pa-lo, tam-pa-lo,
       Follow ma la cus lonelee.

8 "I want you to hoe it with a peacock's feather,"
       Follow ma la cus lonelee,
    "And thresh it all out with the sting of an adder,"
       Ma kee ta lo, kee ta lo, tam-pa-lo, tam-pa-lo,
       Follow ma la cus lonelee.

THE SIX KING'S DAUGHTERS

(CHILD 4, "LADY ISABEL AND THE ELF-KNIGHT")

Numerous versions of this ballad have been found in West Virginia, but in none of these is the knight a preternatural character. He is only a wicked man who promises to marry the lady if she will take some of her parents' money and the two best horses in the stable and ride away with him to Scotland. Sung by Aunt Mary Gainer, Gilmer County.

"Go sad - dle up the two best steeds That stand in your fa-ther's
stall, And a - way to Scot-land we will go. Where mar-ried we will be."

2 She brought him some of her father's gold
   And some of her mother's fee,
   And took him to her father's barn,
   Where horses stood thirty and three.

3 She mounted on the milk-white steed,
   And he on the dapple gray,
   And they rode till they came to the ocean side,
   Three hours before it was day.

4 "O get you down, fair lady," he said,
   "Get ye down, I tell to thee,
   For six king's daughters I have drowned here,
   And the seventh one you shall be.

5 "Take off, take off that costly robe
   And present it unto me,
   For it is a pity such a costly robe
   Should rot in the salt, salt sea."

6 "O turn your face to the willow tree,
   O turn your back to me,
   For it is a pity such a false-hearted man
   A naked woman's body should see."

7 He turned himself around and about,
   His face to the willow tree.
   She gathered him in her lily-white arms
   And threw him in the sea.

8 "O lie you there, you false-hearted man,
   Lie there instead of me,
   For you promised to Scotland we would go,
   Where married we would be."

9 She mounted on her milk-white steed,
   And led the dapple-gray.
   She rode till she came to her father's house
   Two hours before it was day.

THE SEVEN SONS

(CHILD 7, "EARL BRAND" OR "THE DOUGLAS TRAGEDY")

In this tragic ballad Lady Margaret is being forced into a marriage with a man who has title and wealth, but her true love is really Sweet William. The lovers elope in the night and are pursued by Margaret's father and brothers. Sung by Grandfather Gainer.

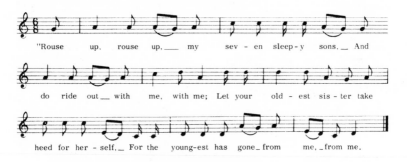

"Rouse up, rouse up,__ my sev-en sleep-y sons,__ And do ride out__ with me, with me; Let your old-est sis-ter take heed for her-self,__ For the young-est has gone_ from me,_from me.

2 "Rouse up, rouse up, my seven bold sons,
   Put on all your armor so bright, so bright,
   For it never shall be said that a daughter of mine
   Has been with Sweet William all night, all night."

3 Sweet William he rode and well he rode,
   Along with his lady away, away,
   Till he saw her seven brothers bold
   And her father riding so gay, so gay.

4 "Get down, get down, Lady Margaret," he said,
   "And hold my horse for a while, a while,
   While I fight with your seven brothers bold
   And your father riding so gay, so gay."

5 She held his horse, she held his horse,
   And did not shed a tear, a tear,
   While she saw her seven brothers fall
   And her father riding up with no fear, no fear.

6 "O hold your hand, Sweet William," she said,
   "O hold your hand for a while, a while;
   It's many a many a sweetheart I could have,
   But a father I could have no more, no more."

7 Her father right up to Sweet William did come,
   And with a drawn sword did fight, did fight;
   Sweet William reined him to the right and the left,
   And pierced the old man through the side, the side.

8 "You can choose for to go," Sweet William he said,
   "You can choose for to go or stay."
   "I'll go, I'll go, Sweet William I'll go,
   For you have left me nowhere to stay, to stay."

9 Sweet William he rode and well he rode,
   Along with his lady so gay, so gay,
   Till he came to his own mother's house,
   And a mother she was alway, alway.

10 "O make my bed, Lady Mother," he said,
   "O make my bed both wide and deep,
   And lay Lady Margaret close by my side
   So that I may sleep, may sleep."

11 Sweet William he died before midnight,
   Lady Margaret died before the day,
   Sweet William died of pure true love,
   Lady Margaret died of sorrow and grief.

THE SISTER'S MURDER

(CHILD 10, "THE TWA SISTERS")

Cox reported three versions of this ballad as having been found up to 1925. Since then we have found numerous versions, all of which generally agree in text and refrain. However, this version is the only one which retains the supernatural element found in most of the Child versions, the use of the murdered sister's hair to make the musical instrument, which revealed the guilt of the murderer when it was played. Sung by Jack Hamrick, Webster County.

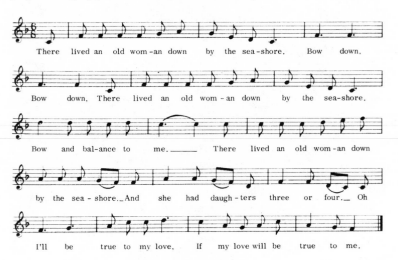

There lived an old wom-an down by the sea-shore. Bow down,

Bow down, There lived an old wom-an down by the sea-shore.

Bow and bal-ance to me._____ There lived an old wom-an down

by the sea-shore.__And she had daugh-ters three or four.__ Oh

I'll be true to my love, If my love will be true to me.

2 A young man came a-courting there.
   Bow down, bow down.
   A young man came a-courting there.
   Bow and balance to me.
   A young man came a-courting there,
   And he made love to the youngest fair.
   Oh I'll be true to my love,
   If my love will be true to me.

10

3 He bought the youngest a fine fur hat.
    Bow down, bow down.
  He bought the youngest a fine fur hat.
    Bow and balance to me.
  He bought the youngest a fine fur hat,
  The oldest sister didn't like that.
    Oh I'll be true to my love,
    If my love will be true to me.

4 "O sister, O sister, let's walk by the shore."
    Bow down, bow down.
  "O sister, O sister, let's walk by the shore."
    Bow and balance to me.
  "O sister, O sister, let's walk by the shore
  And see the ships come sailing o'er."
    Oh I'll be true to my love,
    If my love will be true to me.

5 As they were walking along the sea brim,
    Bow down, bow down.
  As they were walking along the sea brim,
    Bow and balance to me.
  As they were walking along the sea brim,
  The oldest pushed the youngest in.
    Oh I'll be true to my love,
    If my love will be true to me.

6 "O sister, O sister, please lend me your hand."
    Bow down, bow down.
  O sister, O sister, please lend me your hand."
    Bow and balance to me.
  "O sister, O sister, please lend me your hand,
  And I will give you my house and land."
    Oh I'll be true to my love,
    If my love will be true to me.

7 "I'll give you neither my hand nor my glove."
    Bow down, bow down.
  "I'll give you neither my hand nor my glove."
    Bow and balance to me.
  "I'll give you neither my hand nor my glove,
  For all I want is your own true love."
    Oh I'll be true to my love,
    If my love will be true to me.

8 And when they found the young girl fair,
    Bow down, bow down.
  And when they found the young girl fair,
    Bow and balance to me.
  And when they found the young girl fair,
  They made a fiddle bow from her golden hair.
  Oh I'll be true to my love,
  If my love will be true to me.

9 And when on the fiddle the music did sound,
    Bow down, bow down.
  And when on the fiddle the music did sound,
    Bow and balance to me.
  And when on the fiddle the music did sound,
  It cried, "By my sister I was drowned."
  Oh I'll be true to my love,
  If my love will be true to me.

THE BRIDE'S MURDER

(CHILD 11, "THE CRUEL BROTHER")

This tragic ballad has not been reported previously as surviving in West Virginia. This complete version was found in Calhoun County. It was an old family custom that permission of the parents and all older brothers and sisters had to be obtained if a younger member of the family wished to marry. In this case brother Harry was not asked. Sung by Samuel Bennett.

There's three rich maids went out to bleach the cloth, All a - long the ship-yard so

clean, There's three rich men came to court them all, As plain-ly as could be seen.

2 The first rich man was dressed in red,
    All along the shipyard so clean,
He asked if the oldest could him wed,
    As plainly as could be seen.
    (The refrain is repeated in each stanza)

3 The second rich man was dressed in yellow,
    He asked the next if he wasn't a proper fellow.

4 The third rich man was dressed in white,
    He asked the youngest to be his wife.

5 "But you must ask of my father so dear,
    And of my mother who will be near."

6 "And you must ask of my sister Sue,
    Or else your favor you will rue."

13

7 "And don't forget my brother Harry,
Of all men he's the most contrary."

8 The rich man asked of her father dear,
And sought of her mother fairilee.*

9 He asked the favor of her sister Sue,
But forgot her brother so contrary.

10 And all the neighbors far and near,
Came to wish the bride good cheer.

11 Her father led her through the hall,
Her mother dashed before them all.

12 Her sister Sue at her gown did pluck,
And wished her all the best of luck.

13 Her brother Harry waited by the stile,
To greet her for a long, long while.

14 He had a knife both sharp and stout,
And with it he cut her fair white throat.

15 The blood ran down upon her breast,
She knew that hour would be her last.

16 They carried her back to her father's hall,
And there she made her will before them all.

17 "And I leave to my mother there,
All the clothes I have to wear."

18 "And I leave to my sweet Sister Sue,
My rich husband for to view."

19 "And I leave to my brother Harry's wife,
Shame and disgrace for the rest of her life."

20 "And I leave to my brother Harry's son,
To pay the debt his father has won."

*Dialect for "fairly."

14

21 "And I leave to my brother Harry,
   The gallows in payment for his deed."

22 "And may my husband throw the trap,
   Before he stops his tears to shed."

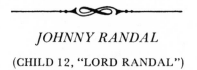

JOHNNY RANDAL
(CHILD 12, "LORD RANDAL")

The usual title for this ballad in West Virginia is "Johnny Randal" or some slight variation, such as "John Randolph." Mr. W. A. Thomas, of Erbacon, Webster County, who sang this version to me, said he knew the Randal family. He said they lived over the mountain. This young man went to see the girl and she fed him poison and he died.

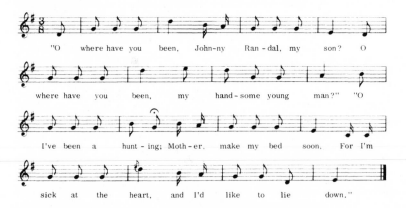

"O where have you been, John-ny Ran - dal, my son? O where have you been, my hand - some young man?" "O I've been a hunt - ing; Moth - er, make my bed soon, For I'm sick at the heart, and I'd like to lie down."

2 "Where got you your dinner, Johnny Randal, my son?
Where got you your dinner, my handsome young man?"
"O I got it at my true-love's; Mother, make my bed soon,
For I'm sick at the heart, and I'd like to lie down."

3 "What did you have for your dinner, Johnny Randal, my son?
What did you have for your dinner, my handsome young man?"
Fried eels in fresh butter; Mother, make my bed soon,
For I'm sick at the heart, and I'd like to lie down."

4 "O I fear you are poisoned, Johnny Randal, my son,
O I fear you are poisoned, my handsome young man."
"O yes, I am poisoned; Mother, make my bed soon,
For I'm sick at the heart, and I'd like to lie down."

5 "What will you leave to your true-love, Johnny Randal, my son?
What will you leave to your true-love, my handsome young man?"
"A rope for to hang her; Mother, make my bed soon,
For I'm sick at the heart, and I'd like to lie down."

THE FATHER'S MURDER

(CHILD 13, "EDWARD")

This ballad is a tragedy, in which a son kills his father because of the counselling of his mother—or, more likely, his step-mother. She thinks that she will be the possessor of her husband's estate and money if the son kills his father, for the son will have to flee from the crime or be hanged. When she sees the blood on the son's sleeve, she thinks the murder has been committed, but she pleads for the son to tell. In the end she receives the curse from the son because of what she had taught him.

Tragic ballads survive in our traditions because of the moral lesson which they teach. Singers often say, after singing a tragic ballad, "There's a mighty good lesson in that song." Sung by W. A. Thomas.

I've no more but he, Oh! I've no more but he." "O

what will you leave to your moth-er dear, Now son, the truth tell me." "The

curse of hell is left to thee, For such you taught to me, oh!"

FAIR FLOWERS IN THE VALLEY

(CHILD 14, "BABYLON")

Ballads are often known by a line of the refrain, as is this one, or by the first line of the song. One does not usually ask a singer for a ballad by title but by telling a summary of the story. As of this writing, this ballad has never before been recorded in West Virginia. Sung by Aunt Polly Gainer, Gilmer County.

There were three sis-ters in the wood. O fair flow'rs in the val - ley. And there they met a rob - ber bold, And the birds they sing so sweet - ly.

2   He showed the eldest a weapon knife,
  O fair flowers in the valley,
 "Will you go with me or lose your life?"
  And the birds they sing so sweetly.
  (The refrain is repeated with each stanza)

3   "O I'd liever that I'd lose my life,
 Before I'll be a robber's wife."

4   Then with his knife so keen and sharp,
 He pierced that maiden through the heart.

5   He showed the second his weapon knife,
 "Will you go with me or lose your life?"

6   "O I'd liever that I'd lose my life,
 Before I'll be a robber's wife."

7   Then with his knife so keen and sharp
 He pierced this maiden through the heart.

8 He showed the youngest his weapon knife,
  "Will you be mine or lose your life?"

9 "O I will never be your wife,
  Nor do I fear to lose my life.

10 "For I have a brother in these woods,
   For many years an outlaw bold.

11 "Before he'd let me be your wife,
   He'd quickly take away your life."

12 "O sister dear, what have I done?
   For now I know I'm your brother John."

13 He put his knife against his heart,
   And from his sister he did part.

IN SCOTLAND TOWN WHERE I WAS BORN

(CHILD 17, "HIND HORN")

Child's "Hind Horn", had never been recorded in West Virginia until it was sung to me by Maggie Hammans Parker, of Marlinton, Pocahontas County, on August 6, 1970. Indeed, no complete version of this ballad has ever been recorded in the United States except in Maine, in 1939.

In Scot-land town where I was born, A la-dy gave to me a ring. "And if this ring stays bright and fair. You'll know that your true love is true, my dear. But if this ring grows old and worn, You'll know that your true love is with some oth-er one."

2 Well, he went on board, and away sailed he,
He sailed till he came to some foreign country.
He looked at his ring, and his ring was worn,
He knew that his true love was with some other one.

3 So he went on board and back sailed he,
He sailed and he sailed to his own country.
One morning as he was a-riding along,
He met with a poor old beggar man.

22

4 "Old man, old man, old man, I say,
   What news have you got for me today?"
   "Sad news, sad news to you I say,
   Tomorrow is your true love's wedding day."

5 "So you can take my riding steed,
   And the beggar's rig I will put on."
   "Well, the riding steed hain't fit for me,
   And the beggar's rig hain't fit for thee."

6 Well, whether it be right or whether it be wrong,
   The beggar's rig he did put on.
   So he begged from the rich, he begged from the poor,
   He begged from the highest to the lowest of 'em all.

7 So he went on at an old man's rate,
   Till he came to the steps of yonder's gate.
   When the bride came trippling down the stair,
   With rings on her fingers and gold in her hair.

8 And a glass of wine to hold in her hand,
   To give to the poor old beggar man.
   He took the glass and drank the wine,
   And in that glass he placed this ring.

9 "O where did you get it, from sea or land,
   Or did you get it from a drownded man's hand?"
   "Neither did I get it from sea or land,
   Nor neither did I steal it from a drownded man's hand.

10 "You gave it to me on our courting day,
   I'll give it back to you on your wedding day."
   Well, off of her fingers the rings she put,
   Off of her hair the gold did fall.

11 "I'll follow my true love wherever he may go,
   If I have to beg my food from door to door."
   Between the kitchen and the hall,
   The beggar's rig he did let fall.

12 His gold a-showing out more fairer than them all,
   He was the fairest of the young men in that hall.
   "I'll follow my true love wherever he may go,
   If I have to beg my food from door to door."

OLD BADMAN

(CHILD 18, "SIR LIONEL")

This Child ballad has been found only in fragmentary form in West Virginia. Not enough of the ballad has been preserved in our traditional song to give the listener even a complete story. It is remarkable that even as much as six stanzas of the song have survived. Sung by Winnie Hamrick, Braxton County.

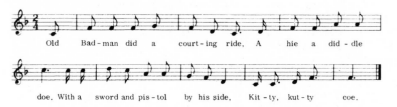

2 Old Badman did a-courting ride,
　　A hie a diddle doe.
　He saw a fine lady in a tree hide,
　　Kitty kutty coe.

3 There is a wild boar in the wood,
　　A hie a diddle doe.
　That will cut your throat to drink your blood,
　　Kitty kutty coe.

4 Old Badman drew his sword so sharp,
　　A hie a diddle doe.
　To cut out this wild boar's heart,
　　Kitty kutty coe.

5 They fought, they fought six hours that day,
　　A hie a diddle doe.
　Till that wild boar did steal away,
　　Kitty kutty coe.

24

6 Old Badman rode to the wild boar's den,
  A hie a diddle doe.
  He saw the bones of a hundred men,
  Kitty kutty coe.

DOWN BY THE GREENWOOD SIDEE

(CHILD 20, "THE CRUEL MOTHER")

We have found Child ballad No. 20 numerous times in West Virginia, with no significant variations in the story. In some versions three babes are born to the unwed mother, but in others, as in this one, there are two babes. In all versions the babes are born in secret in the woods and are immediately murdered by the mother. As she is returning home she sees two pretty babes but does not know they are the ghosts of the babies she has just murdered. Sung by Stella Manthe, Gilmer County.

There was a la-dy who lived in York, O lil-ly and lone-lee, She fell in love with her grand-fa-ther's clerk, Down by the green-wood si-dee.

2 He loved her up and he loved her down,
    O lilly and lonelee,
  He loved her till he filled her arms,
    Down by the greenwood sidee.

3 She placed her foot up against an oak,
    O lilly and lonelee,
  And first it bent and then it broke,
    Down by the greenwood sidee.

4 She placed her foot up against a thorn,
    O lilly and lonelee,
  And there those two little babes were born,
    Down by the greenwood sidee.

5 She had a knife both keen and sharp,
   O lilly and lonelee,
   She pierced those two little babes to the heart,
   Down by the greenwood sidee.

6 She buried them under a marble stone,
   O lilly and lonelee,
   And thought this never would be known,
   Down by the greenwood sidee.

7 As she was going to her grandfather's hall,
   O lilly and lonelee,
   She saw those two little babes playing ball,
   Down by the greenwood sidee.

8 "O babes, O babes, if you were mine,"
   O lilly and lonelee,
   "I'd dress you up in silks so fine,"
   Down by the greenwood sidee.

9 "O mother, O mother, we once were thine,"
   O lilly and lonelee,
   "But you neither dressed us in coarse nor fine,"
   Down by the greenwood sidee.

10 "O babes, O babes, can I ever come there?"
   O lilly and lonelee,
   "No, mother, no, mother, you can't come here,"
   Down by the greenwood sidee.

11 "We'll stand in heaven and ring a bell,"
   O lilly and lonelee,
   "When your poor soul is doomed to hell,"
   Down by the greenwood sidee.

THE TWO CROWS

(CHILD 26, "THE THREE RAVENS")

It is not at all surprising that the West Virginia versions of Child No. 26 are fragmentary, for the versions in Child's work are fragmentary. My grandfather Gainer used to sing this song to me when I was small.

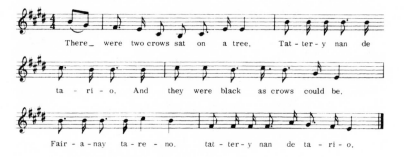

There_ were two crows sat on a tree, Tat - ter - y nan de ta - ri - o. And they were black as crows could be. Fair - a - nay ta - re - no. tat - ter - y nan de ta - ri - o.

2 And the one he said unto his mate,
    Tattery nan de tario,
  "What shall we do for grub to ate?"
    Faira nay tareno, tattery nan de tario.

3 "There lies a man on yonder plain,"
    Tattery nan de tario,
  "Whose body has been lately slain."
    Faira nay tareno, tattery nan de tario.

4 "We'll perch upon his long backbone,"
    Tattery nan de tario,
  "And pick his eyes out one by one."
    Faira nay tareno, tattery nan de tario.

THE RIDDLE SONG

(CHILD 46, "CAPTAIN WEDDERBURN'S COURTSHIP")

Although no complete survival of Child No. 46 has been found in oral tradition in West Virginia, some of the riddles which occur in the old-world ballad are also in the traditional song known as "The Riddle Song." Because of this apparent relationship, we are identifying the "Riddle Song" here so that the student of folk song can make the comparison with Child No. 46. Sung by Mary Bell Workman, Clay County.

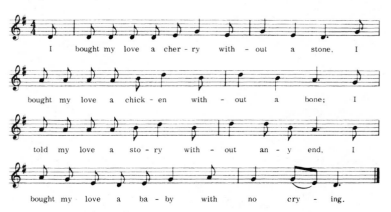

I bought my love a cher-ry with-out a stone, I bought my love a chick-en with-out a bone; I told my love a sto-ry with-out an-y end, I bought my love a ba-by with no cry-ing.

2 How can there be a cherry without a stone?
How can there be a chicken without a bone?
How can there be a story without any end?
How can there be a baby with no crying?

3 Well, a cherry when it's blooming, it has no stone,
A chicken when it's pipping, it has no bone,
The story of our love, it has no end,
A baby when it's sleeping, there's no crying.

OUR YOUNG SON JOHN

(CHILD 49, "THE TWA BROTHERS")

This ballad tells the story of two brothers going to school, and one of them is killed. In one account the death was the result of an accident when they were playfully wrestling and one brother fell on a knife which he was carrying in his pocket. In another version there was a quarrel, and one brother stabbed the other in anger. In this West Virginia version the death is the result of an accident. Sung by Verna Smith, Braxton County.

2 They wrassled up, they wrassled down,
  And Johnnie fell to the ground,
  And out of his pocket there fell a knife
  That fatally wounded his side.

3 "O brother dear, take off my shirt,
  And tear it from gore to gore,
  And place it on my bleeding side
  That it may not bleed no more."

4 His brother, his brother took off his shirt,
  And tore it from gore to gore,
  And placed it on his bleeding side,
  And still it bled the more.

5 "O brother, take me on your back,
And carry me to the churchyard.
Go dig my grave both wide and deep
And easily lay me down."

6 "But what will I tell my papa dear,
When he calls for his young son John?"
"Just tell him I'm in those merry green woods
A-training those hounds to run."

7 "And what will I tell our mama dear,
When she calls for her young son John?"
Just tell her I'm in the high churchyard,
A-learning to read for her."

8 "And what will I tell your sweetheart dear,
When she asks for her sweetheart John?"
"Pray tell her that I'm asleep, asleep,
Pray tell her that I'm asleep."

9 Then his brother dug his grave for him,
And dug it both wide and deep;
He laid his Bible at his head,
And his hymn book at his feet.

LORD BATEMAN

(CHILD 53, "YOUNG BEICHAN" OR "LORD BATEMAN")

This Child ballad is usually known as "Lord Bateman" in America. It is a good love story with a happy ending, in which the real heroic character is a woman. The numbers seven and three in stanza 5 are standard numbers which often occur in folk song and tales. The tune is in the Dorian mode. Maggie Crites, of Braxton County, who knew many old songs, sang this ballad.

Lord Bate-man was an Eng-lish gen-tle-man, He was a lord of high — de - gree; He grew, he grew so dis - con - tent - ed. He vowed he'd sail up - on the sea.

2 Oh, he sailed east, and he sailed west,
   He sailed across the northern sea,
   Until he came to a Turkish country,
   Where he was put in slavery.

3 The Turkish king had a lovely daughter,
   Oh, she was of a high degree,
   She stole the keys from her father's dwelling,
   And out of prison set him free.

4 "Let's make a vow unto each other,
   Let's make it seven long years to stand,
   If you'll not marry another woman,
   I'll never marry another man."

5 Oh, seven long years had passed and gone,
   Seven long years and almost three,
   She gathered up all her fine clothing,
   And vowed Lord Bateman she'd go see.

6 Oh, she sailed east, and she sailed west,
   Until she came to the English shore,
   And there she went to see Lord Bateman,
   She'd vowed she'd love forevermore.

7 "Oh, is this Lord Bateman's hall,
   And is he in there all alone?"
   "Oh, no, oh no," cried the proud porter,
   "Today a bride he's just brought home."

8 "Remind him of the Turkish prison,
   Remind him of the raging sea,
   Remind him of the Turkish lady,
   Who out of prison set him free."

9 "There is a lady at your gate,
   And she is of high degree,
   She wears a ring on her left forefinger,
   And on the others she wears three."

10 Lord Bateman rose up from his table,
   And broke it into pieces three,
   Saying, "I'll give my love to the Turkish Lady
   Who out of prison set me free.

11 "Oh, Lady, take back home your daughter,
   For she is none the worse by me,
   For I will marry the Turkish lady
   Who out of prison set me free."

THE CHERRY TREE

(CHILD 54, "THE CHERRY TREE CAROL")

Since a carol was a song for a particular occasion, usually a religious celebration, this ballad was sometimes called a carol because it was suitable for singing at Christmas time. This was one which my grandfather Gainer used to sing on Sunday mornings.

The sixth day of January was often called "Old Christmas."

When Jo-seph was a young man, a young man was he, He
wed-ded Vir-gin Ma-ry, in the land of Gal-i-lee.

2 When Joseph and Mary were walking one day,
  They walked through an orchard where was cherries to behold.

3 Said Mary to Joseph, so meek and so mild,
  "Please gather me some cherries, for I am with child."

4 Then Joseph flew in anger, in anger he flew,
  "Let the father of that baby gather cherries for you."

5 Then the cherry tree bowed down, low down to the ground,
  And Mary gathered cherries while Joseph stood around.

6 Then Joseph took Mary all on his right knee,
  "Pray tell me, little baby, when your birthday with be."

7 "On the sixth day of January my birthday will be,
  When high in the heavens my star you will see."

DIVERUS AND LAZARUS

(CHILD 56, "DIVES AND LAZARUS")

This ballad has not been reported previously in West Virginia. It is th story of the Gospel parable of The Rich Man and Lazarus, as sung by Au Mary Wilson, of Gilmer County.

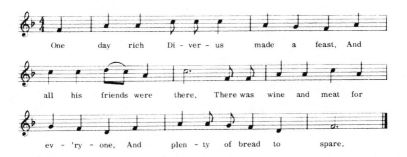

One day rich Di - ver - us made a feast, And all his friends were there, There was wine and meat for ev - 'ry - one, And plen - ty of bread to spare.

2 Poor Lazarus came to Diverus' door,
   And laid him down and down,
   He cried, "Some meat, Brother Diverus,
   Please give unto the poor."

3 "You ain't my brother, Lazarus,
   A-begging at my door,
   I have no meat nor drink for you,
   Nor anything for the poor."

4 Then Diverus sent out his hungry dogs
   To drive poor Lazarus away,
   But the dogs would not bite Lazarus,
   But they licked his sores away.

5 And then it happened on a day
   That poor Lazarus died;
   An angel came from heaven on high
   His soul therein to guide.

6 The angel said to Lazarus,
  "Now come to heaven with me,
  There is a place prepared for you,
  To sit on an angel's knee."

7 And then rich Diverus also died,
  His soul was carried to hell;
  And he must be in awful fire,
  Forever there to dwell.

YOUNG HENEREE

(CHILD 68, "YOUNG HUNTING")

The motivating emotion which causes this tragedy is jealousy. This version was sung to me by Maggie Hammans Parker, of Marlinton, on August 6, 1970.

"Get down, get down, young Hen - er - ee, And stay all night__ with me,_____ And the ver - y best lodg - ing that I can af-ford Will__ be much bet-ter for thee.____

    2 "I won't come, I shan't come in
       And stay all night with you,
       For I have a girl in the merry green lands
       I love much better than you."

    3 She leant herself against a fence,
       And kisses gave him three.
       "That girl you love in the merry green lands,
       She ain't no better than me."

    4 She caught him by the lily-white hand,
       The other'n by the feet,
       She plunged him into the deep blue well
       That was more than a hundred feet.

    5 "Lie there, lie there, young Heneree,
       Till the flesh rots off of your bones,
       That girl you love in the merry green lands
       Will never see you return."

6 There was a pretty parrot bird
  Sitting high on a limb,
  Saying, "You have murdered young Heneree,
  And in the well thrown him."

7 "Come down, come down, my pretty parrot bird,
  And sit on my right knee,
  Your cage shall be of the finest gold,
  And decked with ivory."

8 "I won't come down, I can't come down,
  I won't come down," says she,
  "For you have murdered young Heneree,
  And you would murder me."

LORD THOMAS AND FAIR ELLENDER

(CHILD 73, "LORD THOMAS AND FAIR ANNET")

This is one of the old-world ballads most frequently found in West Virginia tradition. We have found numerous variations of the title, the best known being "Lord Thomas and Fair Ellender." However, there are no significant variations in the story. The phrase "brown girl" indicates that the girl had brown hair. The Germanic tradition favored blonde girls as being truly fair. Sung by Aunt Mary Wilson.

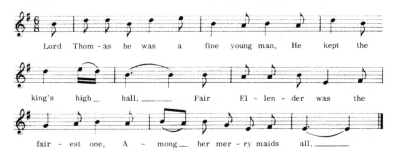

Lord Thom-as he was a fine young man, He kept the king's high hall, Fair El-len-der was the fair-est one, A-mong her mer-ry maids all.

2 "O Mother, O Mother, come riddle us all,
Come riddle us all in one,
And say shall I marry fair Ellender,
Or bring the brown girl home?"

3 "The brown girl has a house and lot,
Fair Ellender she has none;
My dearest son, take my advice,
And bring the brown girl home."

4 "O Father, O Father, come riddle us all,
Come riddle us all in one,
And say shall I marry fair Ellender,
Or bring the brown girl home?"

5 "The brown girl has both oxen and cows,
   Fair Ellender she has none;
   My own dear son, take my advice,
   And bring the brown girl home."

6 Lord Thomas he mounted his milk-white steed,
   And rode to Fair Ellender's hall;
   No one was so ready as Fair Ellender,
   To arise and bid him walk in.

7 "What news, what news, Lord Thomas?" she said,
   "What news have you brought to me?"
   "I've come to ask you to my wedding."
   "That's very bad news," said she.

8 "Come, Father and Mother, I'll ask you both,
   I'll ask you both as one,
   Whether shall I go to Lord Thomas' wedding,
   Or tarry with thee at home?"

9 "There may be many of your friends,
   And many of your foes,
   And if you'll take warning from such good friends,
   You'll tarry with me at home."

10 "There may be many of my friends,
   And many of foes,
   But for them all I shall not care,
   To Lord Thomas' wedding I'll go.'

11 She dressed herself in scarlet red,
   Her maids were dressed in green,
   And every town that she rode through
   They took her to be some queen.

12 She rode till she came to Lord Thomas' hall,
   She loudly called to him.
   No one was so ready as Lord Thomas himself
   To arise and bid her walk in.

13 He took her by the lily-white hand,
And led her through the hall,
And set her down at the head of the table
Among his ladies all.

14 "Is this your bride, Lord Thomas?" she said,
"I think she is wondrous brown;
When you could have married as fair a lady
As ever came into this town."

15 "Throw none of your slurs," Lord Thomas said,
"Throw none of your slurs at me;
Much better do I love your little finger
Than the brown girl's whole body."

16 The brown girl had a little pen-knife,
It was both keen and sharp;
Between the long ribs and the short
She pierced Fair Ellender's heart.

17 "O what is the matter?" Lord Thomas said,
"What makes you look so pale?
You once did wear as fresh a color
As anyone in your day."

18 "O are you blind, Lord Thomas?" she said,
"Or can't you very well see?
O can't you see my own heart's blood
Come trickling to my knee?"

19 He took the brown girl by the hand,
And led her into the hall,
And with his sword cut off her head
And kicked it against the wall.

20 Then placing the handle against the wall,
The point against his breast,
Saying, "Here lie the bodies of three young lovers,
Lord send their souls to rest.

21 "Go dig my grave in the roses sweet,
Go dig it both wide and deep,
And lay Fair Ellender by my side,
And the brown girl at my feet."

FAIR MARGARET AND SWEET WILLIAM

(CHILD 74, "FAIR MARGARET AND SWEET WILLIAM")

This tragic love ballad ordinarily retains its old-world title in our tradition. It has been found frequently in West Virginia. It is pretty clear in the beginning of the song that Lady Margaret thinks she is to be the bride of Sweet William. The shock of seeing William with his bride causes her to die. There was an old belief that if one kissed the lips of the dead, he, too, would die soon. William, overcome by sorrow, kissed the lips of Margaret (stanza 10) knowing that he, too, would die. The plants that grow up from the graves symbolize the eternal unity of lovers. Sung by "Aunt" Mattie Long, Braxton County.

Sweet William he rose one merry, merry morn, And dressed himself in blue; "Pray tell to me that long, long talk Between Lady Margaret and you."

2 "I know nothing of Lady Margaret," he said,
   "Lady Margaret knows nothing of me;
   Before eight o'clock tomorrow morn
   A wedding you will see."

3 Lady Margaret was standing by her diamond window,
   A-combing her long yellow hair;
   Who did she spy but Sweet William and his bride,
   As they went along the road so fair?

4 Down, down she threw her ivory comb,
And back she tossed her hair,
And down she fell from her diamond window,
Nevermore was seen standing there.

5 "Such dreams, such dreams I never had,
I'm afraid they will prove true.
I dreamed that my room was full of white swine,
And the love tears came flowing true."

6 He rode till he came to Margaret's house,
And he jingled all on the ring;
And who was so willing than her seventh brother rose
To rise and let him in.

7 "O is she in the kitchen?" he said,
"Or is she in the hall?
Or is she in the upper room
Among the fair ladies all?"

8 "She's neither in the kitchen," he said,
"Neither is she in the hall;
She's in her coffin made of lead,
With her pale face turned to the wall."

9 "Roll down, roll down, those milk-white sheets,
Roll down, roll down those blinds,
And let me kiss those red rosy cheeks
As often as they've kissed mine."

10 Once he kissed her snowy white breast,
And once he kissed her chin,
Three times he kissed her cold, cold lips
That pierced his heart within.

11 Lady Margaret she died on Monday morn,
Sweet William he died tomorrow;
Lady Margaret she died for pure true love,
Sweet William he died for sorrow.

12 Lady Margaret was buried under one willow tree,
Sweet William under another;
Out of Lady Margaret's grave there sprang a rose,
Out of Sweet William's a brier.

13 They grew and they grew till the church steeple high,
And they could not grow any higher.
Their branches they spread and their leaves they met,
And they tied in a true lover's knot.

LORD LOVEL

(CHILD 75, "LORD LOVEL")

"Lord Lovel" has been found numerous times in West Virginia, and it retains its old-world title almost without exception. There are very few textual variations, and the tunes are very much the same for all versions. Grandfather Gainer sang this version.

Lord Lov - el stood at his cas - tle gate, A comb-ing his milk-white steed, __ When up came La - dy Nan - cy Bell, To wish __ her lov- er good speed, good speed, To wish __ her lov - er good speed. __

2 "O where are you going, Lord Lovel?" she said,
"O where are you going?" said she.
"I'm going away, Miss Nancy Bell,
Strange countries for to see, to see,
Strange countries for to see."

3 "When will you be back, Lord Lovel?" she said,
"When will you be back?" said she.
"A year or two or three at the most,
I'll return to my Lady Nancee, Nancee,
I'll return to my Lady Nancee."

4 He had not been gone but a year and a day,
Strange countries for to see,
When languishing thoughts came into his head,
Lady Nancy Bell he would go see, go see,
Lady Nancy Bell he would go see.

5　So he rode and he rode, he rode and he rode,
　　Till he came to London Town,
　　And there he heard Saint Patrick's bells,
　　And the people all mourning around, around,
　　And the people all mourning around.

6　"O what is the matter?" Lord Lovel he said,
　　"O what is the matter?" said he.
　　"A lady is dead," the people all said,
　　"And they call her the Lady Nancee, Nancee,
　　And they call her the Lady Nancee."

7　He ordered the grave to be opened wide,
　　And the shroud to be let down,
　　And then he kissed the pale, pale face,
　　And the tears came a-trickling down, down, down,
　　And the tears came a-trickling down.

8　Lady Nancy she died as it might be today,
　　Lord Lovel he died on the morrow.
　　Lady Nancy she died for pure, pure grief,
　　Lord Lovel he died from sorrow, sorrow,
　　Lord Lovel he died from sorrow.

9　Lady Nancy was buried in the churchyard,
　　Lord Lovel he lay in the choir,
　　And out of her bosom there grew a red rose,
　　And out of her lover's a brier, a brier,
　　And out of her lover's a brier.

10　They grew and they grew to the church steeple top,
　　Till they couldn't grow up any higher,
　　Then they twined themselves in a true lover's knot,
　　For all true lovers to admire, admire,
　　For all true lovers to admire.

SWEET ANNIE OF ROCK ROYAL

(CHILD 76, "THE LASS OF ROCH ROYAL")

Of all the tragic ballads, this one is perhaps the saddest. After Annie make the long trip in her ship to find the father of her baby, she "pulls at the string" of George's door. This string was the latchstring which held the pin that bolted the door. We are not sure whether George's mother believes that Annie is really an imposter and the son should be protected, or if it is a case of a jealous mother. This ballad has not survived well in our traditions, and we are fortunate to find this complete survival sung by Mrs. Lula Gardner, of Nicholas County.

"O who will shoe my bon-nie feet, And who will glove my_ hands? And who will tie my_ waist so_ neat With the new-made Lon-don band?"

2 "O who will comb my yellow hair
With the bright new silver comb?
O who will be daddy to my boy
Till my lover George come home?"

3 Her father will shoe her bonnie feet,
Her mother gloved her hands,
Her sister tied on her waist so neat
The new-made London band.

4 Her cousin combed her yellow hair
With the bright new silver comb,
But heaven knew the daddy of her boy
Till her lover George came home.

5 Her father gave her a new ship
   And led her to the sand,
   She took her boy up in her arms,
   And sailed away from the land.

6 On the sea she sailed and sailed,
   For over a month or more,
   Till she landed her new ship
   Near to her lover's door.

7 Long she stood at her lover's door,
   And long pulled at the string,
   Till up got his false mother,
   Saying, "Who pulls at the string?"

8 "O it's Annie of Rock Royal,
   Your own come o'er the sea,
   With your own dear son held in her arms,
   So open the door to me."

9 "Be off, be off, you bold woman,
   You come not here for good,
   You are only a strumpet or a bold witch,
   Or else a mermaid from the sea."

10 "I'm not a witch nor a strumpet bold,
   Nor a mermaid from the sea,
   But I am Annie of Rock Royal,
   So open the door to me.

11 "So open the door to me, dear George,
   And open it with speed,
   Or your young son here in my arms
   With the cold will soon be dead."

12 "If you be Annie of Rock Royal,
   Though I know not you may be,
   What pledge can you give to me
   I ever kept your company?"

13 "O don't you mind, dear George?" said she,
   "When we were drinking wine,
   How we gave the rings from our fingers,
   And how the best was mine?

14 "Though yours was good enough for me,
    It was not so good as mine,
    Yours was made of bright red gold,
    While mine had a diamond fine.

15 "So open the door to me, dear George,
    And open it with speed,
    Or your young son here in my arms
    With the cold will soon be dead."

16 "Away, away, you bold woman,
    Take from my door your shame,
    For I have got another true love,
    And you may hasten home."

17 "And if you have gotten another true love,
    After all the oaths you swore,
    O here is farewell to you, false George,
    For you will never see me more."

18 Slowlye, slowlye went she back
    As the day began to dawn;
    She set her foot on her new ship,
    And bitterly did mourn.

19 George started up all in his sleep,
    And quick to his mother he said,
    "O I dreamed a dream tonight, mother,
    That made my heart so sad.

20 "I dreamed that Annie of Rock Royal
    Was jingling at the pin,
    She had our young son in her arms,
    But none would let her in."

21 "O a bold woman stood there at the door,
    With a child all in her arms.
    But I wouldn't let her come in the house
    For fear she would work you a charm."

22 Quicklye, quicklye got he up,
    And fast he ran to the sand,
    And there he saw his Annie dear
    A-sailing from the land.

23 And "Hey, Annie!" and "Ho, Annie!
   O listen, Annie, to me!"
   But the louder he cried for Annie,
   The louder roared the sea.

24 The wind blew high, the sea grew rough,
   The ship was broken in two,
   And soon he saw his sweet Annie
   Come floating o'er the waves.

25 He saw his young son in her arms,
   Both tossed about by the tide,
   He pulled his hair and he ran fast,
   And he plunged in the sea so wild.

26 He caught her by the yellow hair,
   And drew her out on the sand,
   But cold and stiff were her snowy limbs,
   Before he reached the land.

27 O he has mourned over sweet Annie
   Till the sun was going down,
   Then with a sigh his heart did burst,
   And his soul to heaven has flown.

THE THREE LITTLE BABES

(CHILD 79, "THE WIFE OF USHER'S WELL")

The most common title of this ballad in West Virginia tradition is "The Three Little Babes." It has been found many times. In another version which I have recorded, which will appear in a subsequent volume, the three babes tell their mother, "The tears that were shed by you, dear mother, have wet our winding sheet." An old superstition was that if one mourned too much for the dead, the spirit could not rest in peace but would return to earth. Sung by Mrs. Lou Pritt, Gilmer County.

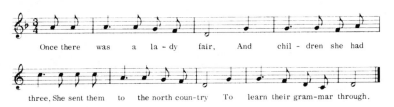

Once there was a la-dy fair, And chil-dren she had three, She sent them to the north coun-try To learn their gram-mar through.

2 They had not been there very long.
   Not more than three weeks to a day,
   When grim death came running 'round,
   And took those babes away.

3 She set the table long and wide,
   Prepared with bread and wine,
   "Come eat and drink, my three little babes,
   Come eat and drink of mine."

4 "We do not want your bread," they cried,
   "Nor do we want your wine,
   For yander stands our Savior Lord,
   And in Him we all design."

5 She made the bed in the backmost room,
   And trimmed it in fine sheets,
   And on the top put a golden spread,
   Where they had often slept.

6 "Take it off, take it off," cried the eldest one,
   "Take it off, take it off," cried he,
   "For yander stands our Savior Lord,
   And to Him we all must go."

7 They then stepped out all robed in white,
   And upward they did fly;
   They flew away on eagle wings
   To live with God on High.

LITTLE MATHIE GROVES

(CHILD 81, "LITTLE MUSGRAVE AND LADY BARNARD")

In West Virginia this ballad is sometimes known as "Lord Donel's Wife," or "Lord Arnold's Wife." The moral lesson is clear: the act of an unfaithful wife results in tragedy. The indelicate details of the story are justified because of the lesson which is taught. This version was sung by Verna Smith, of Braxton County.

Lit-tle Math-ie Groves he went to church, To see and to be seen, He placed him-self be - side the door, For to see the la-dies walk in.

2 Well the first came in was a raven black,
 The next came in was a brown,
 The next came in was Lord Donel's wife,
 The gayest of the town.

3 She turned herself around and about,
 She turned herself to me,
 She placed her eyes on Little Mathie Groves,
 And these very words said she.

4 She placed her eyes on Mathie Groves,
 And these very words said she:
 "I will take you home with me tonight,
 This very night," said she.

5 "O I dare not, O I dare not,
 I dare not for my life,
 For I know by the rings on your right hand
 You are Lord Donel's wife."

6 "It makes no difference whose wife I am,
  To you or to no other man,
  For my husband he is not at home,
  He is in some distant land."

7 The little foot-page was a-standing by,
  And he heard every word was said;
  He swore Lord Donel should hear of this,
  Before it was break of day.

8 Oh he had sixteen miles to go,
  And ten of them he run,
  He run till he came to the broke-down bridge,
  Then he held his breath and swum.

9 He swum till he came to the other side,
  Then he took to his heels and run,
  He run till he came to the king's castle,
  And he tapped at the bell and it rung.

10 "What news, what news, my little foot-page,
   What news have you brought to me?
   Are there any of my castles a-blowing down,
   Or any of my men false be?"

11 "There's none of your castles a-blowing down,
   Nor none of your men false be,
   But little Mathie Groves is at your home
   In bed with your lady."

12 "If this be a lie you have brought to me,
   And a lie I believe it to be,
   I'll build me a gallows so strong and high,
   And hanged on it you shall be."

13 "If this be a lie I have brought to you,
   And a lie you find it to be,
   You need not build no gallows, sir,
   You can hang me to a tree."

14 "If this be the truth you have brought to me,
   But a lie I think it to be,
   I've just one daughter in this wide world,
   And your bride she soon shall be.

54

15 "Go saddle me the milk-white horse,
   Go saddle me the brown,
   Go saddle me the swiftest horse
   That ever stood on ground."

16 He called his men all in a row,
   And he picked out his three;
   He marched them away to a Scottish home,
   This happy couple for to see.

17 But there was one among the three
   That owed little Mathie good will;
   He put his bugle to his face
   And blew it loud and shrill.

18 "Hush, hush," little Mathie says to her,
   "Hush, I must go,
   For Lord Donel is coming home,
   I heard his bugle blow."

19 "Lie still, lie still," the lady says,
   "And keep me from the cold,
   For it's only my father's shepherd boy
   A-leading his sheep to the fold."

20 She turned him over and give him a kiss,
   And soon they fell asleep;
   But when they awoke again
   Lord Donel was at their feet.

21 "O how do you like my curtains, sir,
   And how do you like my sheets,
   And how do you like my lady fair
   Who lies in your arms asleep?"

22 "Very well I like your curtains, sir,
   Very well I like your sheets,
   But the best of all is your lady fair,
   Who lies in my arms asleep."

23 "Get up from there, put on your clothes,
   And fight me like a man,
   For when I'm dead no one can say
   I've slain a naked man."

24 "How can I get up, put on my clothes,
And fight you like a man,
When you have got two well-grown swords,
And me not a pocket knife?"

25 "I know I have got two well-grown swords,
And they cost me deep in the purse,
But I'll give to you the best of them,
Myself shall take the worst.

26 "You can strike the very first lick,
And strike it like a man,
And I will strike the very next lick,
I'll kill you if I can."

27 Little Mathie Groves struck the very first lick,
He struck a fearful blow,
But when Lord Donel struck his lick,
Little Mathie couldn't do no more.

28 He took his fair lady by the hand,
He set her upon his knee.
He said, "Which of all do you love best,
Little Mathie Groves or me?"

29 "Very well I like your red rosy cheeks,
Very well I like your chin,
But I wouldn't give Mathie Groves' fingernail
For Lord Donel and all his kin."

30 He took her by the hair of the head,
He drug her over the floor,
And with his sword cut off her head,
As he had done little Mathie before.

31 He put the sword against the wall,
The point against his heart,
He gave a loud scream and a squall,
Lord Donel and his wife must part.

BARBARA ALLEN

(CHILD 84, "BONNY BARBARA ALLEN")

Of all the old-world ballads surviving in West Virginia, "Barbara Allen" is the best known. There are several different tunes for this ballad, but the following one is probably the oldest tune in existence. It was preserved in the traditions of the Gainer family, who came from Ireland in 1725. The ballad was sung to me by Aunt Mary Wilson, my grandfather's sister.

In Scar - let Town where I was born,— There was a fair maid dwel - ling, Made ev - 'ry youth cry, "Well a - way," And her name was Bar - bry— Al - len.

2 'Twas early in the month of May,
　When the green buds were a-swellin',
　Young Johnny Green on his death-bed lay
　For the love of Barbry Allen.

3 He sent his servant to the town
　Where his love was a-dwellin',
　Saying, "Follow me to my master, dear,
　If your name be Barbry Allen."

4 So slowly, slowly she got up,
　And slowly she went nigh him,
　But all she said when she got there,
　"Young man, I think you're dyin'."

5 "O don't you remember the other night,
  When you were at the tavern?
  You drank a health to the ladies round,
  But slighted Barbry Allen."

6 "O yes, I remember the other night,
  When I was at the tavern,
  I drank a health to the ladies round,
  But gave my love to Barbry Allen."

7 As she was walking through the town,
  She heard the death bell tollin',
  And ev'ry toll it seemed to say,
  "Hard-hearted Barbry Allen."

8 "O Mother, O Mother, go make my bed,
  Go make it soft and narrow,
  Young Johnny Green died for me today,
  And I'll die for him tomorrow."

9 O she was buried in the old churchyard,
  And he was buried a-nigh her,
  And out of her grave grew a red, red rose,
  And out of his a green brier.

10 And they grew till they reached to the top of the church,
   And they couldn't grow any higher;
   And there they met in a true-lover's knot,
   The red rose and the green brier.

YOUNG COLLINS

(CHILD 85, "LADY ALICE")

The story is not quite clear as to the cause of the death of Young Collins, but Fair Elinor's washing of the white marble stone seems to be an omen. In stanza 5, Elinor kisses the lips of her dead lover, in spite of the fact that this means death for her, too. It was an ancient folk belief that if one kissed the lips of the dead, the living person would soon die. The lily growing out of Young Collins' breast and touching the breast of Fair Elinor is a symbol of the eternal power of love, with nature expressing a sympathy with the lovers. There are many instances of this "pathetic fallacy" in folk song and story. Sung by B. B. Chapman, Webster County.

Young Col-lins rode out one eve-ning, While the trees and the flow'rs were in

bloom, And there he saw Fair El - i - nor, A - wash-ing a white mar-ble stone. _

2 "If I should die this very night,
   Which I feel in my own heart I will,
   Go bury me under the white marble stone
   At the foot of Fair Elinor's green hill."

3 Fair Elinor sat in her own cottage door,
   All dressed in her laces so fine;
   'Twas there she saw a coffin go by,
   As bright as her own eyes could shine.

4 "Whose coffin, whose coffin, whose coffin?" she cried,
   "Whose coffin is this I see?"
   " 'Tis young Johnnie Collins' clay cold corpse,
   An old true lover of thine."

5 She ordered the coffin to be opened right there,
  And they placed it on the ground,
  And there she kissed his clay cold lips,
  While the tears came trickling down.

6 "O lay him down, O lay him down,
  Down on the grass so green,
  For tomorrow when the sun goes down
  Fair Elinor a corpse will be seen."

7 They buried Fair Elinor in the east,
  And Young Collins in the west,
  And out of Collins' breast there grew a lily,
  That touched Fair Elinor's breast.

8 And out of the north there blew a cold wind,
  That split the lily in two;
  A thing that never was seen before,
  And never will be seen again.

HARRY SAUNDERS

(CHILD 87, "PRINCE ROBERT")

This ballad has never previously been reported as being found in West Virginia. It is a tragic story in which a mother poisons her son because she does not approve of the girl he marries. Sung by Mrs. Nan Wilson, Nicholas County.

It's for - ty miles to Ni-cut Town, The near-est way you go, But Har - ry Saund -ers has tak- en a wife, That he dares not to bring home.

2 His mother called to her hired girl,
"Sally, draw me a cup of tea,
For I see my son Harry's coming
To eat a meal with me."

3 His mother lifted the cup of tea,
And touched her lips to the drink,
But never a drop of the poison cup
Of drinking did she take.

4 Harry took the cup of tea
And put it to his mouth,
And he opened his bright red lips,
And the poison went quickly down.

5 His wife sat at Nicut Hill,
Waiting for Harry to come;
She called to her own sister dear,
"Has my husband now come home?"

6 She went up to her room
And put on a riding skirt.
She went out to the stable old
And saddled her roan steed.

7 But when she came to Harry's home,
The guests were all in the hall.
The hearse was standing by the yard,
And the friends were mourning all.

8 "I've come for none of his gold," she said,
"Nor none of his lands so wide."
"The watch and chain I've thrown in the well,
From his own sweet bride to hide."

9 And then she kissed his cold white cheeks,
And then she kissed his chin,
And then she kissed his bright red lips
Where there was no breath come in.

10 And then she fell upon the floor,
Her head against the bier,
Her heart did break, it was so sore,
But she shed not any tear.

BOLAKIN

(CHILD 93, "LAMKIN")

This is an incomplete version of the Child ballad "Lamkin," but the fragment we have found does agree with the old-world story. Bolakin is a stonemason who does not receive payment for building the lord's castle. He gets revenge by killing the lord's child. Bolakin became a name in oral tradition to frighten young children when they became unruly. Sung by Aunt Polly Gainer.

2 Bolakin came to the castle gate,
  Where he saw the lord's child at play.
  He seized the child by the neck,
  And carried him away.

3 They found the child's body by the road,
  His life had been taken away.
  But Bolakin was never seen again,
  He's alive to this day, they say.

THE GALLOWS TREE

(CHILD 95, "THE MAID FREED FROM THE GALLOWS")

In the summer of 1959, as I was driving along a country road at Dry Creek, Raleigh County, I met Andrew Burnside driving his pick-up truck. I knew him as a good fiddle player, and I was surprised when he volunteered to sing this ballad.

"O hang-man, hang-man, Hold your rope, Hold it for a while, For I think I see my fa-ther com-ing, 'Way off man-y a mile; O Fa-ther, Fa-ther, have you brought me gold. Gold for to pay my fee? Or have you come to see me hung Up - on the gal-lows tree?" "No, daugh-ter I've not brought you gold, Gold for to pay your fee, For I have come to see you hung Up - on the gal-lows tree."

2 "O hangman, hangman, hold your rope,
 Hold it for a while,
 For I think I see my mother coming
 'Way off many a mile.
 Mother, Mother, have you brought me gold,
 Gold for to pay my fee?
 Or have you come to see me hung
  Upon the gallows tree?"

"No, daughter, I've not brought you gold,
Gold for to pay your fee,
For I have come to see you hung
    Upon the gallows tree."

3 "O hangman, hangman, hold your rope,
Hold it for a while,
For I think I see my brother coming
'Way off many a mile.
O Brother, Brother, have you brought me gold,
Gold for to pay my fee?
Or have you come to see me hung
    Upon the gallows tree?"
"No, sister, I've not brought you gold,
Gold for to pay your fee,
For I have come to see you hung
    Upon the gallows tree."

4 "O hangman, hangman, hold your rope,
Hold it for a while,
For I think I see my true-love coming
'Way off many a mile.
O True-love, True-love, have you brought me gold,
Gold for to pay my fee?
Or have you come to see me hung
    Upon the gallows tree?"
"Yes, True-love, I have brought you gold,
Gold for to pay your fee,
For I've not come to see you hung
    Upon the gallows tree."

THE BAILEY DAUGHTER OF HAZELENTOWN
(CHILD 105, "THE BAILIFF'S DAUGHTER OF ISLINGTON")

This ballad had never been found in the traditions of West Virginia until "Aunt" Mattie Long, of Gassaway, sang it to me in the summer of 1950. She was eighty-two years old at the time. She said she learned the song when she was a girl.

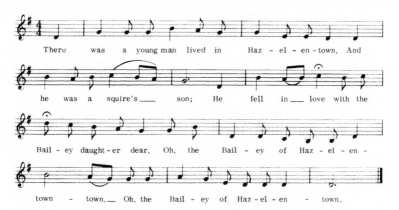

There was a young man lived in Haz-el-en-town, And he was a squire's___ son; He fell in___ love with the Bail-ey daught-er dear, Oh, the Bail-ey of Haz-el-en-town — town,___ Oh, the Bail-ey of Haz-el-en — town.

2 They sent him away to some foreign country
  For to study and improve his mind;
  They sent him away to some foreign country,
  And to leave his for-true-love behind, —hind,
  And to leave his for-true-love behind.

3 It was all on one fine holiday
  When the maids all went out for to play;
  They all went out but the Bailey daughter dear,
  And so cunningly she stole away, —way,
  And so cunningly she stole away.

66

4 She traveled on twelve months and one day,
  When a-riding along the highway,
  Oh, who should she meet but her own true-love,
  Came a-riding along the highway, —way,
  Came a-riding along the highway.

5 She stepped right up to this young man,
  Caught his horse by the bridle rein,
  "One penny, one penny, kind sir," said she,
  "For to ease a poor troubled mind, mind,
  For to ease a poor troubled mind."

6 "O where were you bred, my pretty little maid?
  O where were you bred and born?"
  "In Hazelentown, kind sir," said she,
  "Where I've borne a many a scorn, scorn,
  Where I've borne a many a scorn."

7 "Do you know anything of the Bailey daughter dear,
  Whether she be dead or alive?"
  "Oh, she is dead, for she is not alive,
  And was buried twelve months ago, —go,
  And was buried twelve months ago."

8 "O take away my milk-white steed,
  My saddle, whip, and bow;
  And I will away to some foreign country
  Where no one else be known, known,
  Where no one else be known."

9 "O she is not dead, for she is yet alive,
  And standing by your side,
  O she is not dead, for she is yet alive,
  Just ready for to be your bride, bride,
  Just ready for to be your bride."

THE DUKE'S DAUGHTER

(CHILD 155, "SIR HUGH" OR "THE JEW'S DAUGHTER")

Numerous versions of this ballad have been found in West Virginia, varying only slightly in details. Some versions are called "The Jew's Daughter," suggesting anti-Semitism. The anti-Semitism, however, has been erased by the folk tradition. I have heard old people pronounce "Jew" as "Due," which might explain the title, "The Duke's Daughter." Sung by Mrs. Rogers, of Newton, Roane County.

It rained a mist, it rained a mist, It rained all o-ver the town,__ When three lit-tle boys went out to play, And tossed their ball a-round, a-round, And tossed their ball a-round.__

2 And first they tossed the ball too high,
   And then it was too low,
   Until into the Duke's garden it went,
   Where no one dared to go, to go,
   Where no one dared to go.

3 Out came the Duke's daughter all dressed in silk,
   All dressed in silk so fine.
   "Come in, come in, my pretty sweet boy,
   You shall have your ball again, again,
   You shall have your ball again."

4 "I won't come in, I shan't come in,
   Without my playmates do,
   For I have heard whoever comes in

Will never come out again, again,
Will never come out again."

5 First she showed him a big red apple,
And then a soft ripe pear,
And then a cherry red as blood,
To entice this little boy in, in, in,
To entice this little boy in.

6 First she led him into the parlor,
And then out into the hall,
And then into the dining room,
Where no one could hear him call, call, call,
Where no one could hear him call.

7 She wrapped him in a napkin stout,
And pinned it with a pin.
She called up for the butcher knife
To let his heart's blood out, out, out,
To let his heart's blood out.

8 "O spare me now, O spare me now,"
The little boy did cry,
"And when I grow to be a man
My riches shall be thine, be thine,
My riches shall all be thine.

9 "O lay the Bible at my feet,
The prayerbook at my head,
And when my playmates ask for me,
Go tell them that I'm asleep, asleep,
Go tell them that I'm asleep."

MARY HAMILTON

(CHILD 173, "MARY HAMILTON")

"Mary Hamilton" is not well known in West Virginia tradition. I have heard it sung by young "folk singers," usually with guitar or autoharp accompaniment, who have learned the song from other "folk singers" by way of records and radio. The following version from Nicholas County is incomplete, but enough of the story is told to reveal to the listener that Mary Hamilton has thrown her illegitimate baby into the sea and she is hanged for the murder. Sung by Pearl Bell.

Word has gone through the kitch-en, And word has gone through the hall, __ That

Ma-ry Ham-il-ton goes with child To the high-est stew-ard of all. ___

2 She tied it in her apron,
   And threw it in the sea,
   Saying, "Lie you there, you little babe,
   For you'll never see more of me."

3 The old queen came to Mary,
   She heard the baby cry,
   Then Mary was taken before the judge,
   And there condemned to die.

4 Mary stood at the gallows high,
   She never shed a tear.
   The people came to see her die,
   From her lips these words they did hear.

70

5 "Last night there were four Marys,
  Tonight there'll be but three,
  There was Mary Seaton, and Mary Beaton,
  And Mary Carmichael and me."

THE GYPSY DAVY

(CHILD 200, "THE GYPSY LADDIE")

Most of the versions of this ballad found in West Virginia tradition have the title "The Gypsy Davy." The words of the first stanza indicate that the gypsy Davy puts a charm on the lady by his singing, so that she is willing to go with him even though it means deserting her husband and baby. Sung by Blanche Kelley.

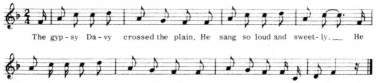

The gyp-sy Da-vy crossed the plain, He sang so loud and sweet-ly. __ He sang till he made the green woods ring. To charm the heart of a la-dy.

2 The lord of the house came home that night,
   Inquiring for his lady;
   The servants said on every hand,
   "She's gone with the gypsy Davy."

3 "Go saddle up my milk-white steed.
   The black is not so speedy,
   And I will ride all day and night
   To overtake my lady."

4 He mounted on his milk-white steed,
   The one that was so speedy,
   He rode all day and he rode all night,
   Till he overtook his lady.

5 "Have you forsaken your house and lands,
   Have you forsaken your baby?
   Have you forsaken your own true-love,
   And gone with the gypsy Davy?"

72

6 "Yes, I've forsaken my house and lands,
   And I've forsaken my baby;
   Yes, I've forsaken my own true-love
   To go with the gypsy Davy."

7 The lord went home alone that night,
   Went home without his lady;
   She'd rather sleep beneath the stars
   In the arms of the gypsy Davy.

BESSIE BELL AND MARY GRAY

(CHILD 201, "BESSIE BELL AND MARY GRAY")

*This sad little ballad tells of two ladies who built a house out in the
country to escape from a plague, but the disease was brought to them,
and they had to be buried away from the graveyard of their kin. Sung
by Ivy Lee Myers.*

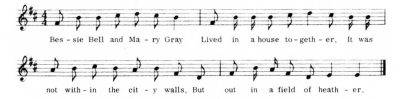

Bes - sie Bell and Ma - ry Gray   Lived   in   a house to - geth - er.   It was

not with - in   the   cit - y   walls,   But   out   in   a field   of   heath - er.

2 And while the plague was raging round,
   They thought it would pass them by,
   But death soon came in through the door,
   These ladies had to die.

3 They could not lie in their own churchyard,
   Among their next of kin,
   But a grave was dug close by their house
   To lay these ladies in.

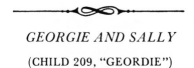

GEORGIE AND SALLY

(CHILD 209, "GEORDIE")

In the Scottish version of this ballad, Geordie is ransomed and returns home with his wife, but in this West Virginia version Georgie is hanged for his crimes. Sung by Moses Ayers.

As I walked out on Mon-day morn, On Mon-day morn-ing ear - ly,

There I spied a pret-ty fair maid, La - ment-ing for her Geor - gie.

2 Georgie he's done some famous deeds,
   Such deeds and crimes a many,
   He's stole sixteen of the King's choice steeds,
   And sold them in Bohamia.

3 "Go saddle me the milk-white steed,
   For the brown is not so speedy,
   For I must go to the King's high court,
   To plead for the life of Georgie."

4 The King looked over his right shoulder,
   And thus he said to Sally,
   "Pretty fair maid, you've come too late,
   For he's condemned already."

5 The King looked over his left shoulder,
   And thus he said to Georgie,
   "May the Lord have mercy on you,
   For you've confessed and you must die."

75

6 And Georgie he marched down the hall,
  Where he took leave of many,
  When he took leave of his own true love,
  It grieved him worst of any.

7 And Georgie was hung by a golden cord,
  A cord that had never hung any,
  For his father he was a noble lord,
  And his mother was a noble lady.

THE BANKS OF YORROW

(CHILD 214, "THE BRAES O YARROW")

We have recovered only this fragment of three stanzas of this Scottish ballad rare in oral tradition in West Virginia. "Aunt" Mattie Long, of Gassaway, sang it and said she was sorry that she could not remember all of the song, which she had learned when she was a girl. Aunt Mattie's great-grandfather came to America from Scotland before the Revolutionary War and fought in the Revolution.

"O do not go a-way from me, My true love, do not go, For I dreamed last night that you'd be killed, When you did leave me so."

2 "O I must go tonight, my love,
    Even though you sorrow,
    For I told your brothers I'd meet them there,
    Upon the banks of Yorrow."

3 Her brothers waited there for him,
    As he went down to Yorrow,
    They slew him there just as they planned,
    And left his wife in sorrow.

THE RANTIN' LADDIE

(CHILD 240, "THE RANTIN LADDIE")

This ballad is rare in West Virginia tradition. This version is closely related to Child version B. Sung by Alpheus Danley, Gilmer County.

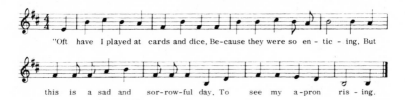

"Oft have I played at cards and dice, Because they were so en-tic-ing, But this is a sad and sor-row-ful day, To see my a-pron ris-ing.

2 "My father he does but slight me,
And my mother she does scorn me,
And all my friends make light of me,
And all the servants sneer at me.

3 "Oft have I played at cards and dice,
For the love of my laddie,
But now I must sit at my father's fireboard
And rock my bastard baby.

4 "But had I one of my father's servants,
For he has so many,
That will go to the eastern shore
With a letter to the rantin' laddie."

5 "Here is one of your father's servants,
For he has so many,
That will go to the eastern shore
With a letter to the rantin' laddie."

6 "When you get there to the house,
To the eastern shore so bonnie,
With your hat in your hand bow low down to the ground
Before the company of the rantin' laddie."

7 When he got there to the house,
To the eastern shore so bonnie,
With his hat in his hand he bowed down to the ground,
Before the company of the rantin' laddie.

8 When he looked the letter o'er,
So loud he burst out laughing,
But before he read it to the end,
The tears they were down dropping.

9 "O who is this, O who is that,
Who has been so ill to my Maggie?
O who is this has been so bold,
So cruel to treat my lassie?"

10 "Her father will not know her,
And her mother she does but scorn her,
And all her friends do make light of her,
And all the servants they do sneer at her."

11 "Four-and-twenty milk-white steeds,
Go quick and make them ready,
As many gay lads to ride on them
To go and bring home my Maggie.

12 "Four-and-twenty bright brown steeds,
Go quick and make them ready,
As many bold knights to ride on them
To go and bring home my Maggie."

13 Ye lasses all where'er ye be,
If ye lie with an eastern shore laddie,
Ye'll happy be, ye'll happy be,
For they are fresh and free.

THE HOUSE CARPENTER'S WIFE

(CHILD 243, "JAMES HARRIS" OR "THE DAEMON LOVER")

Almost all of the numerous West Virginia survivals of this ballad are called "The House Carpenter," or "The House Carpenter's Wife." A young woman has a lover who goes to sea, and she waits in vain for his return. She finally marries a house carpenter and they have a baby. Then her former lover returns, claiming that he is rich, and entices her to leave with him. She weeps for her little baby, but she cannot return. After three weeks on sea the ship sinks mysteriously. In some versions the story makes it very clear that it is the ghost of her lover who returns to take her away from her husband. Sung by Aunt Mary Wilson.

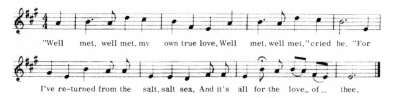

"Well met, well met, my own true love, Well met, well met," cried he, "For I've re-turned from the salt, salt sea, And it's all for the love of thee.

2 "Well, I could have married a king's daughter dear,
   I'm sure she'd have married me,
   But I've returned from the salt, salt sea,
   And it's all for the love of thee."

3 "Well, if you could have married a king's daughter dear,
   I'm sure you are to blame,
   For I have married a house carpenter,
   And indeed he's a fine young man."

4 "If you will leave your house carpenter,
   And go along with me,
   I'll take you where the grass grows green
   On the banks of Italy."

5 "What have you got to maintain me on,
  Or keep me from slavery?"
  "I've seven ships that's just passed o'er,
  And seven more on sea."

6 Then she took up her sweet little babe,
  And gave it kisses three,
  Saying, "Stay at home with your pappy,
  And keep him company."

7 They had not been on sea two weeks,
  I'm sure it was not three,
  When this young lady began to weep,
  And she wept bitterly.

8 "O do you weep for gold," said he,
  "Or do you weep for store,
  Or do you weep for that sweet little babe,
  That you'll never see any more?"

9 "I do not weep for gold," cried she,
  "Nor do I weep for store,
  But I do weep for that sweet little babe
  That I'll never see any more."

10 They had not been on sea three weeks,
  I'm sure it was not four,
  When the ship sprang a leak in the middle of the deep,
  And it sank to rise no more.

HENRY MARTIN

(CHILD 250, "HENRY MARTYN")

This ballad is rare in West Virginia tradition. Cox has one version, found in 1916. Sung by L. P. Williams, Ritchie County.

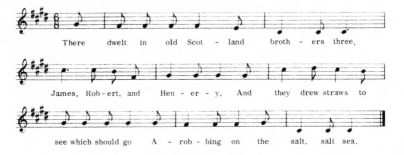

There dwelt in old Scot - land broth - ers three, James, Rob - ert, and Hen - er - y, And they drew straws to see which should go A - rob - bing on the salt, salt sea.

2 The short straw fell to Henery,
    The youngest of the brothers three,
    That he should go in the ship on the sea
    To rob for all his brothers and he.

3 Henery sailed out from the shore,
    All one night upon the sea,
    When he met a great and mighty ship
    A-sailing there across the sea.

4 Henery Martin drew close by her.
    "I beg you now to let us go."
    "No, no, by God, that will I not,
    No, that I will never do."

5 Henery Martin said all to them,
    "And you cannot sail by me,
    For I have gone in a ship on the sea
    To rob for all my brothers and me."

6 Broadsides on each other they gave,
  They fought for all of hours three,
  Until Henery Martin got a death wound,
  And sank down in the deep, deep sea.

THE LADY NEAR NEW YORK TOWN

(CHILD 272, "THE SUFFOLK MIRACLE")

This ballad is rare in West Virginia tradition. It appeared in Folk Songs of the South *in 1925, but Dr. Cox states that the incident of the handkerchief being tied around the head of the corpse has never been found in any West Virginia version. Our complete version which follows was sung by Mrs. Nancy Webb, of Raleigh County, in 1954. She said she had learned the song from her mother.*

The beautiful young woman falls in love with a farmer boy against her parents' will. They send her away three hundred miles or more to live with her uncle so that she will forget her lover. Twelve months later her lover calls for her on horseback to take her home. She gladly goes with him, riding on the horse behind him. When he complains of a headache, she ties her handkerchief around his head. When she kisses him she says his lips are colder than clay. When they arrive at her father's house, the lover disappears, and when the grave of the lover is opened, the corpse is found with the handkerchief tied around his head.

2 By chance there came a farmer's boy,
Who gained her love with all great joy.
When her two parents came to know,
They sent her three hundred miles or more.

3 "Your mother's clothes, your father's steed,
   I've come for thee all in great speed."
   And as her uncle understood,
   He thought it might be for her good.

4 So he helped her all on behind him,
   They traveled swifter than the wind.
   But before they reached her father's gate,
   He did complain his head did ache.

5 She pulled out her handkerchief,
   And bound it around about his head.
   She kissed his lips and then did say,
   "My love, they're colder than the clay.

6 "When we get home, good fires we'll have."
   But little did she know he was from his grave.
   And about three hours or a little bit more,
   She rapped all on her father's door.

7 Her father rose, put on his clothes,
   "You're welcome home, dear child," says he,
   "You're welcome home, dear child," says he,
   "But what kind friend has come with thee?"

8 "Did you not send that loving man?"
   "That man, that man, he can love no more!"
   And to know he had been twelve months dead,
   This made the hair raise on his head.

9 He summoned a judge and a jury too,
   They opened the coffin of him to view.
   And they knew that he had been twelve months dead,
   But there was that handkerchief around his head.

10 Come all you people, both young and old,
   And love your children dearer than gold,
   And let your children have their way,
   For now you see love won't decay.

THE DRUNK HUSBAND

(CHILD 274, "OUR GOODMAN")

There are various titles for the West Virginia survivals of this ballad, but the one most used is "The Drunk Husband." Some versions of the ballad tend to lapse into vulgarity, but this version is simply a good, humorous story which should not offend any singer or listener. Sung by Edgar Taggart, Gilmer County.

The old man came home the oth-er night as drunk as he could be, He saw a horse out in the barn where his horse ought to be. Sing a fa la did-dle-i-day.

2 "My dear wife, my darling wife, O what is this I see?
   Whose horse is that out in the barn where my horse ought to be?"
       Sing a fa la diddle-i-day.

3 "You old fool, you blind fool, can't you plainly see?
   It's nothing but the heifer calf my mother sent to me."
       Sing a fa la diddle-i-day.

4 "I've traveled many thousand miles over land and sea,
   But a saddle on a heifer calf I never before did see."
       Sing a fa la diddle-i-day.

5 The old man came home the other night as drunk as he could be,
   He saw a hat upon the rack where his hat ought to be.
       Sing a fa la diddle-i-day.

6 "My dear wife, my darling wife, O what is this I see?
   Whose hat is that upon the rack where my hat ought to be?"
   Sing a fa la diddle-i-day.

7 "You old fool, you blind fool, can't you plainly see?
   It's nothing but the milk crock my mother sent to me."
   Sing a fa la diddle-i-day.

8 "I've traveled many thousand miles over land and sea,
   But a feather on a milk crock I never before did see."
   Sing a fa la diddle-i-day.

9 The old man came home the other night as drunk as he could be,
   He saw a coat hang on the wall where his coat ought to be.
   Sing a fa la diddle-i-day.

10 "My dear wife, my darling wife, O what is this I see?
    Whose coat is that hangs on the wall where my coat ought to be?"
    Sing a fa la diddle-i-day.

11 "You old fool, you blind fool, can't you plainly see?
    It's nothing but the coverlid my mother sent to me."
    Sing a fa la diddle-i-day.

12 "I've traveled many thousand miles over land and sea,
    But buttons on a coverlid I never before did see."
    Sing a fa la diddle-i-day.

13 The old man came home the other night as drunk as he could be,
    He saw a head lie on the couch where his head ought to be.
    Sing a fa la diddle-i-day.

14 "My dear wife, my darling wife, O what is this I see?
    Whose head is that upon the couch where my head ought to be?"
    Sing a fa la diddle-i-day.

15 "You old fool, you blind fool, can't you plainly see?
    It's nothing but a cabbage head my mother sent to me."
    Sing a fa la diddle-i-day.

16 "I've traveled many thousand miles over land and sea,
    But a mustache on a cabbage head I never before did see."
    Sing a fa la diddle-i-day.

GET UP AND BAR THE DOOR

(CHILD 275, "GET UP AND BAR THE DOOR")

This ballad, preserved in family tradition for many generations, brought laughter to the family circle on many a long winter evening. It was sung by W. A. Thomas, Webster County.

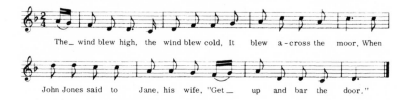

The_ wind blew high, the wind blew cold, It blew a-cross the moor, When John Jones said to Jane, his wife, "Get_ up and bar the door."

2 "Oh, I have worked all day," said she,
"I've washed and scrubbed the floor,
You lazy man, get up, I say,
Get up and bar the door."

3 "Oh, I have worked so hard," said he,
"I know I can't do more;
So come, my own, my dearest wife,
Get up and bar the door."

4 Then they agreed between the two,
A solemn oath they swore,
That the one who spoke the very first word
Would have to bar the door.

5 The wind blew east, the wind blew west,
It blew all over the floor,
But neither one would say a word
For barrin' of the door.

6 Three robbers came along that way,
     They came across the moor;
     They saw a light and walked right in,
     Right in through the open door.

7 "Oh, is the owner of this house
     A rich man or a poor?"
     But neither one would say a word
     For barrin' of the door.

8 They ate the bread, they drank the ale,
     Then said, "Come, give us more."
     But neither one would say a word
     For barrin' of the door.

9 "Let's pull the old man's beard," said one,
     "Let's beat him till he's sore."
     But still the old man wouldn't speak
     For barrin' of the door.

10 "I'll kiss his pretty wife," said one,
     "Oh, her I could adore."
     And then the old man shook his fist
     And gave a mighty roar.

11 "Oh, you'll not kiss my wife," said he,
     "I'll throw you on the floor."
     Said she, "Now, John, you've spoken first,
     So get up and bar the door."

DANDOO

(CHILD 277, "THE WIFE WRAPT IN WETHER'S SKIN")

This ballad survives in West Virginia under various titles: "Dandoo," "The Old Woman Who Wouldn't Work," and "The Woman and the Sheep's Skin." It is almost always sung with an intricate nonsense refrain, which adds much to the humor of the ballad. Sung by Mr. W. K. Knight, Doddridge County.

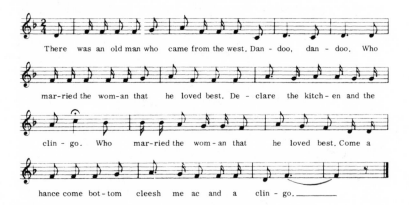

There was an old man who came from the west. Dan - doo, dan - doo. Who mar-ried the wom-an that he loved best. De - clare the kitch - en and the clin - go. Who mar-ried the wom-an that he loved best. Come a hance come bot - tom cleesh me ac and a clin - go.

2 This old man came in from the plow.
        Dandoo, dandoo.
    Says, "Wife, is my breakfast ready now?"
    Declare the kitchen and the clingo.
    Says, "Wife, is my breakfast ready now?"
    Come a hance come bottom cleesh me ac and a clingo.

3 "There are some dumplings in the pot."
        Dandoo, dandoo.
    "You can eat them now while they are hot."
    Declare the kitchen and the clingo.
    "You can eat them now while they are hot."
    Come a hance come bottom cleesh me ac and a clingo.

4 This old man went to his fold.
   Dandoo, dandoo.
   He skinned a wether fat and old.
   Declare the kitchen and the clingo.
   He skinned a wether fat and old.
   Come a hance come bottom cleesh me ac and a clingo.

5 He put the skin on his wife's back.
   Dandoo, dandoo.
   And with a stick went whicketty whack.
   Declare the kitchen and the clingo.
   And with a stick went whicketty whack.
   Come a hance come bottom cleesh me ac and a clingo.

6 "I'll tell my father and all my kin."
   Dandoo, dandoo.
   You whip me on my naked skin."
   Declare the kitchen and the clingo.
   "You whip me on my naked skin."
   Come a hance come bottom cleesh me ac and a clingo.

7 "You can tell your father and all your kin."
   Dandoo, dandoo.
   "That I'm only tanning my wether's skin."
   Declare the kitchen and the clingo.
   "That I'm only tanning my wether's skin."
   Come a hance come bottom cleesh me ac and a clingo.

8 Since then she's been a very good wife.
   Dandoo, dandoo.
   And I hope she'll be to the end of her life.
   Declare the kitchen and the clingo.
   And I hope she'll be to the end of her life.
   Come a hance come bottom cleesh me ac and a clingo.

THE FARMER'S WIFE AND THE DEVIL

(CHILD 278, "THE FARMER'S CURST WIFE")

This was Granny's "favorite" funny ballad. When the ballad was sung, the nonsense refrain became a very practical singing device, for while the refrain was being sung, the listeners could laugh and still not lose any of the story in the lines that followed. Granny's name was Phoebe Gainer; she lived in Gilmer County.

There was an old man lived un-der the hill, If he ain't moved a-way he's liv-ing there still. Sing fie-did-dle-i, did-dle-i, fie-did-dle-i, did-dle-i-day.

2 Old Satan came to the man at the plow,
    Said, "One of your family I'm goin' to have now."
      Sing fie-diddle-i, diddle-i, fie-diddle-i, diddle-i day.
      (The refrain is repeated in each stanza)

3 "O, it's not your son that I do crave,
    But it's your old wife I'm goin' to have."

4 "O Satan, take her with all my heart,
    I hope, by golly, you'll never part."

5 Old Satan took her upon his back,
    He carried her away like an old miller's sack.

6 When he got her to the forks of the road,
    Says he, "Old woman, you're an awful load."

7 When he got her to the gates of hell,
   Says, "Stir up the fire, we'll scorch her well."

8 Ten little devils came rattling their chains,
   She upped with her stick and knocked out their brains.

9 And the little devils began to squall,
   "Take her home, pappy, she'll kill us all."

10 Old Satan took her back to the old man,
   Says, "Keep her at home now if you can."

11 When she got home the old man was in bed,
   She upped with her stick and knocked him in the head.

12 Said he, "Old woman, did you fare well?"
   Said she, "Old man, I flattened all hell."

13 Now you can see just what these women can do,
   They can whip men and devils, too.

14 Now there's one advantage women have over men,
   They can go to hell and come back again.

THE WISE FARMER

(CHILD 283, "THE CRAFTY FARMER")

One version of this ballad, printed by Cox in 1925, was contributed in 1916. Apparently no tune was recovered. My grandfather Gainer sang this ballad.

One day a farmer was riding alone, Riding along the high-way, A robber stepped out in the road, And thus to him did say.

2 "Old man, you should not ride alone,
   For there are thieves a many,
   They'll rob from you all that you have,
   And not leave you a penny."

3 "If they should stop me on the road,
   I'm sure they'll not get any,
   For I've hidden it in my saddle bags,
   It's safe there every penny."

4 The robber said, "I'll take it now,
   Your money, Sir, I'll take it."
   The farmer took the saddle bags
   And threw them over the hill.

5 When the robber got down off his horse,
   After the bags to scurry,
   The farmer took the robber's horse
   And rode off in a hurry.

6 When he opened the robber's bag,
  There was wealth a plenty,
  For he found a hundred pounds of gold,
  And silver ten times twenty.

THE GOLDEN WILLOW TREE

(CHILD 286, "THE SWEET TRINITY," OR "THE GOLDEN VANITY")

This ballad is well-known in our tradition. It is sometimes called "Sailing In the Lowlands Low." It is a tragic story in which the captain of the ship fails to keep his word to the cabin boy, who is left to drown in the sea. Sung by Charles Ayers, Gilmer County.

There was a noble ship and it sailed upon the sea, And it went by the name of the Golden Willow Tree, As it sailed in the Lowlands low, low, low, As it sailed in the Lowlands low.

2 There was another ship and it sailed upon the sea,
   And it went by the name of the Turkish Revelee,
   As it sailed in the Lowlands low, low, low,
   As it sailed in the Lowlands low.

3 Then up spoke the Captain and said, "What will it be?
   Oh, how can we sink that Turkish Revelee?
   As she sails in the Lowlands low, low, low,
   As she sails in the Lowlands low."

4 Then up spoke the cabin boy, and up spoke he,
   Saying, "What will I receive if I sink her in the sea?
   As she sails in the Lowlands low, low, low,
   As she sails in the Lowlands low."

5 "O I will give you gold and I will give you fee,
   And you may have my daughter your bride for to be,
   If you sink her in the Lowlands low, low, low,
   If you sink her in the Lowlands low."

6 He leaped into the sea and away swam he,
   He swam till he came to the Turkish Revelee,
   As she sailed in the Lowlands low, low, low,
   As she sailed in the Lowlands low.

7 Then out of his pocket an auger he drew,
   He bored seven holes and let the water through,
   As she sailed in the Lowlands low, low, low,
   As she sailed in the Lowlands low.

8 Some were playing cards and some were playing checks,
   But soon they were in water all up to their necks,
   As they sailed in the Lowlands low, low, low,
   As they sailed in the Lowlands low.

9 He fell upon his breast and away swam he,
   And he swam back again to the Golden Willow Tree,
   As she sailed in the Lowlands low, low, low,
   As she sailed in the Lowlands low.

10 Saying, "Captain, O Captain, please take me back on board,
   O Captain, I hope that you will keep your word,
   As we sail in the Lowlands low, low, low,
   As we sail in the Lowlands low."

11 "O no, sir, O no, sir, I can't take you on board,
   O I can't be so kind as to keep a foolish word,
   As we sail in the Lowlands low, low, low,
   As we sail in the Lowlands low.

12 He fell upon his breast and away swam he,
   And bade a sad farewell to the Golden Willow Tree,
   As she sailed in the Lowlands low, low, low,
   As she sailed in the Lowlands low.

THE MERMAID

(CHILD 289, "THE MERMAID")

This ballad is rare in West Virginia tradition. Details of the story are lacking, but in the first stanza there are two omens that predict the sinking of the ship: the beginning of the voyage on Friday, and the sighting of a mermaid. Both of these are bad omens. Sung by Dennis Wease, Calhoun County.

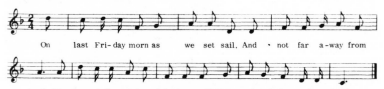

On last Fri-day morn as we set sail, And · not far a-way from
land, The Cap-tain he spied a fair mer-maid, With comb and glass in her hand.

2 O the storm and the winds do blow, blow, blow,
   O the raging winds do roar,
   And us three sailors a-climbing to the top,
   And the landmen a-lying below.

3 The first came up was the captain bold,
   And a jolly old man was he.
   "O this very night in merry Engalond,
   A wife is waiting for me."

4 The next came up was the ship's little boy,
   A fine little boy was he.
   "O this very night in merry Engalond
   A mother is waiting for me."

5 The next came up was a greasy, greasy cook,
   A greasy old cook was he.
   "I care more for the kettles and the pots
   Than I do for the roaring of the sea."

98

The next came up was a seaman bold,
   A bold seaman was he.
   "For the want of a boat we shall all be drowned
   And sunk in the salt, salt sea."

7 Then round and round went the gallant ship,
   Three times around went she,
   And the very last time she turned around
   She sank in the salt, salt sea.

PRETTY SARAH

(CHILD 295, "THE BROWN GIRL")

There will be folklorists who will dispute my claim that this ballad is a variant of Child No. 295-B. However, the similarities in the two ballads are so striking that I believe I am correct. This version, which we found in Nicholas County, tells a good story, although the language in some stanzas suggests a broadside origin. The lady who sang it, Mrs. Maggie Crites, said she learned it long ago from her parents.

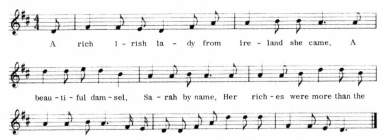

A rich I-rish la-dy from Ire-land she came, A beau-ti-ful dam-sel, Sa-rah by name, Her rich-es were more than the king could pos-sess, And her beau-ti-ful be-hav-ior was worth all the rest.

2 At once a young doctor a-courting her came,
This beautiful damsel, Sarah by name,
He courted her for six months, I'll tell you the truth,
This beautiful damsel, this beautiful youth.

3 "O Sarah, O Sarah, O Sarah," said he,
"If it's that in love we cannot agree,
For you are too brown for me," said the young man,
"I'll find one with beauty as soon as I can."

4 Oh, seven months had passed and gone,
When this young man fell sick at last,
And tangled in love he knew not why,
He sent for his damsel he once did deny.

5 "Are you the young doctor sent for me here,
Or am I the doctor can kill or can cure?"
"Oh, yes, you're the doctor can kill or can cure,
And without your assistance I cannot endure.

6 "O Sarah, O Sarah, O Sarah," said he,
"Don't you remember when I courted thee?"
"But then you denied me and left me forlorn,
And now I'll reward you with hatred and scorn."

7 "For what's past and gone, love, forget and forgive,
And grant me some longer time here to live."
"No, I won't forgive you as long as I have breath,
But I'll dance on your grave when I'm under the earth."

8 Then off from his finger a gold ring he drew,
Saying, "Wear this ring, Sarah, when you dance over me,
Let your colors shine brighter where'er you are seen,
When you are dancing, Sarah, the queen."

THE SOLDIER AND THE MAID

(CHILD 299, "TROOPER AND THE MAID")

It is with much hesitancy that I include this Child ballad survival in this volume. It has not flourished in our tradition, for it is not the kind of ballad that would be sung in the home in the presence of children. Indeed, when Professor George Kittredge edited Child's work in a one-volume edition for student use, he omitted this ballad. However, in these times it is not likely that many students of folklore will consider this ballad too indelicate for their listening or reading. I did not find it in a barroom or on the courthouse square, but it was sung to me by a very dear old lady, Maggie Crites, who also sang beautiful old hymns.

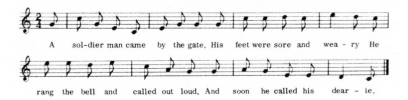

A sol-dier man came by the gate, His feet were sore and wea - ry He rang the bell and called out loud, And soon he called his dear - ie.

2 The hired girl saw him from the door,
The moon was shining clearly,
She said, "Young man, you're welcome here,
You're welcome here, my dearie."

3 She took him by his big broad hand,
And led him to the table.
She gave him bread and meat to eat,
As much as he was able.

4 "Dear honey, tonight I'll lie with you,
Tonight with you I'm sleeping,
And I'll make your fat sides shake
Before I leave you in the morning."

102

5 She went upstairs and made the bed,
   Just as it was for a lady,
   She jerked off her dress and petticoat,
   Saying, "Soldier, are you ready?"

6 Then they played for a long, long while,
   Till of playing they were weary,
   They fell asleep in each other's arms,
   Till the sun was shining clearly.

7 The first time that the bugle played
   Was, "Up, up, and away, man,"
   The second time the bugle played,
   Was, "The morn's the battle day, man."

8 "Sweetheart, I must leave you now,
   Sweetheart, I must leave you,
   But when I come this way again,
   I will stop in and see you."

9 "When shall we two meet again,
   When shall we meet and marry?"
   "When cockle shells be silver bells,
   No longer, love, we'll tarry."

PART TWO
Other Ballads and Folk Songs

A ballad is a song that tells a story. We have found many ballads in the oral traditions of singers in the West Virginia hills which are not surviving variants of the ballads which Child included in his work, *The English and Scottish Popular Ballads.* Many of these are of old-world origin, and some originated in America. The origins of many of them 'are unknown. Some of the works which Child rejected as not being genuine traditional ballads, did later become genuine folk ballads by passing into oral tradition and surviving as folk songs.

Of the thirty-two songs in the following section of this volume, eighteen are ballads. Only one of these ballads is of old-world origin, "The Drummer Boy of Waterloo," though some of the others may be adaptations of earlier old-world ballads. The ballad of "St. Clair's Defeat" has a tune which is undoubtedly of old-world origin, but the words are obviously American.

Singing was a part of the daily lives of the people. Grandmother sang as she sat at the spinning wheel, and mother sang as she went about the work of the home. Grandfather sang as he worked about the place or as he sat on the porch in the summer twilight. There was a song to express every human feeling or desire: the hunger to escape to a land of adventure with knights and ladies; the desire to preserve a good lesson taught by a story of tragedy; the desire to express a religious feeling; the need for laughter; the need for love—there was a song needing no accompaniment but the beating of the human heart. Of the eighteen ballads in this section, nine tell stories of tragedy, while six are humorous.

As I look back to the days of my own childhood and youth, my clearest memories are of the singing that I heard in our home and community. Somewhere in the intervening years I have picked up some poetic lines, the author of which I have forgotten, and which I have undoubtedly altered, which recall those long summer evenings after the work was done:

> That time of day as soft as gray wool yarn,
> While mother insects trilled their lullabies,
> We sat together on the porch.
> Farmwise, my grandparents knew that a child's heart,
> Like a barn, has lofts and crannies waiting to be stored.
> And from the green fields of their own upbringing,
> They filled my heart with lilting old-time singing.
> Now, on days when I am feeling sad or bored,
> My joy returns on some old ballad winging.

WHAT SHALL I GIVE TO THEE?

Aunt Mary Wilson sang this song and told this story: Mary Fisher and her mother were sitting in the front room of their home one day, when Mrs. Fisher looked out the window and said, "Mary, there comes that old witch woman up the path through the meadow. Now, if she comes here, don't let her pick up anything and take it away with her for she'll put a spell on us." When the old woman came to the door, Mrs. Fisher said to her, "Now, we don't want you in our house, for you're a witch and we know it." The old woman went away in a huff and walked down by the garden. She leaned over and picked a leaf of lettuce from a lettuce bed that Mary had planted. She waved the lettuce leaf and laughed as she went away.

Soon after that Mary took sick and they couldn't do a thing for her. They knew that she'd been witched. Mary used to sing a lot, and the song that she sang most before she died was "What Shall I Give To Thee?"

What shall I give to thee? Dear, we must part Some-thing to hide a-way, Close to the heart. Give me an i - vy leaf, fresh from the vine, give me an i - vy leaf, green as the pine.

2 What shall I give to thee? Life is so strange;
   All I could offer thee surely must change.
      Give me an ivy leaf, fresh from the vine,
      Give me an ivy leaf, green as the pine.

A FEW MORE MONTHS

When I went to "Uncle" Frank Kennedy's home in Gilmer County it was twilight time, and I found Mr. Kennedy sitting alone outside the house. When I told him I was trying to write down the old songs, and I would like to hear him sing the song that I'd heard people say he sang, Uncle Frank replied, "Well, it's a mighty fine thing you are doing, for the young people are not learning the old songs. I can't sing the way I used to, but I'd like for you to hear the song." He sang softly, seemingly almost oblivious to my presence.

A few more months, A few more years, A few more pray'rs, A few more tears, It won't be long, A few more years will hush my song, My earth-ly song, When they shall lay me in the val-ley.

2 A little pain, a little joy,
   Just less or more, it matters not,
   Some mingling yet with earth's alloy,
   And then forgot, Oh, soon forgot,
       When they shall lay me in the valley.

THE WEST VIRGINIA FARMER

Mr. Henry B. Bryant, who made fine "dulcimores" and sold them for twelve dollars, in 1950 sang this humorous song to me about the West Virginia farmer who has to work hard to grow anything on the rocky hillsides. Mr. Bryant said his mother sang a lot of songs.

He played the "dulcimore" with much skill, but he never used the instrument to accompany the songs. He lived in Nicholas County.

Oh, the West Vir-gin-ia hills, with their man-y rocks and rills, Where the farm-er has to scratch a-way to see his gran-'ry filled, In the morn-ing up he jumps, And a-mong the rocks and stumps, All a-long the hot and sul-try day he hums. Scratch a-way, scratch a-way, On the hot and sul-try-day. In the hot and sul-try eve-ning scratch a-way, And when the day is done, At the set-ting of the sun, He can feed his horse a lit-tle bite of hay.

2 In the early days of spring,
   To his clearing he must cling,
   And never think of pleasure-time or any such a thing;
   He must chop and split and burn,

And make every crook and turn,
To see his patch of ground a crop of gray.

Work away, work away,
In the hot and sultry day,
In the hot and sultry evening work away;
And when the day is done,
At the setting of the sun,
He can feed his horse a little bite of hay.

3 When the sun is shining hot
And of rest he thinketh not,
He swings his scythe with vigor in his stony meadow lot;
Till a "jacket" pops his nose,
And to double size it grows,
Then he stops a while to rub the itching spot.
Rub away, rub away, in the hot and sultry day,
All the balance of the evening rub away,
And when the day is done,
At the setting of the sun,
He can feed his horse a little bite of hay.

4 In the early days of fall
That bring vigor to us all,
When the farmer pulls his punkins and his hogs begin to call;
When he finds them sick and dead
With the cholera in the head,
Then his happy dreams of sausage turn to gall.

Call away, call away,
On the frosty autumn day,
With tears in his peepers hear him call;
And when the day is done,
And he hath not found a one,
He concludes he hasn't got a pig at all.

5 Now the winter's come at last,
Brings the snow so thick and fast,
That this foolish farmer thinks that he will get some rest at last;
But he very quickly sees
He must get some wood or freeze,
There's work again, and summer days are past.

Work away, work away,
On the cold winter day,
On the cold winter evening work away;
And when the sun has set,
And his nose and chin have met,
He can feed his horse a little bite of hay.

JOHN HENRY

*John Henry is one of West Virginia's great folk heroes, who became
the champion of the working man against the machine at the Big Bend
Tunnel on the Chesapeake and Ohio Railroad in 1870-73. The railroad
tracks had been constructed along the Greenbrier River to Talcott, West
Virginia, where the river makes a big bend. Since the distance could be
shortened greatly by tunneling through the mountain, it was decided to
build the tunnel, beginning in 1870. The work of drilling into the solid
rock had to be done by hand, one man holding and turning the drill
while another man struck the drill with a sledge hammer. This man was
called a "steel driver." One day a man came to the "Captain" of the
job, saying he had a steam drill that could do the work of many men.
The captain said that he would buy the machine if it could beat his best
steel driver, John Henry. A contest was held and according to the song,
John Henry beat that steam drill by three inches, but he died with his
hammer in his hands. Sung by Mrs. Warren Mullins, Nicholas County.*

2 John Henry said to his Captain,
"I ain't nothing but a man,
But before I'll let your steam drill beat me down,
I'll die with my hammer in my hand, Lord, Lord,
I'll die with my hammer in my hand."

3 John Henry got a thirty pound hammer,
Beside the steam drill he did stand.

He beat that steam drill three inches down,
And he died with his hammer in his hand, Lord, Lord,
He died with his hammer in his hand.

4 John Henry had a little woman,
Her name was Julie Ann,
She went down the track never lookin' back,
Says, "John Henry, you have always been a man, Lord, Lord,
John Henry, you have always been a man."

5 They took John Henry to the graveyard,
And they buried him in the sand,
And ev'ry time that train comes roaring by,
Says, "There lays a steel-drivin' man, Lord, Lord,
There lays a steel-drivin' man."

JOHN HARDY

John Hardy is another West Virginia song about a man in McDowell County, West Virginia, who killed a man in a card game in a coal company camp. He was hanged at Welch in January, 1894.

Because of the similarity of the names John Henry and John Hardy, and because some versions of the songs confuse the two names, there are some who think that these two men were the same person. Adding to the confusion is the fact that both men were black and both worked on the railroad. However, there is no doubt that they were two distinct men. (See L. W. Chappell, John Henry, A Folklore Study, 1933.) Sung by Ernest Danley, Gilmer County.

John Har - dy was a bad, bad man, He came from a bad, bad land. He killed a man in the Shaw-nee Camp, And he's too ner - vy for to run, good Lord! And he's too ner - vy for to run.

2 John Hardy was standing in the dice-room door,
   Not taking any interest in the game,
   When along came a girl, threw five dollars down,
   Saying, "Deal John Hardy in the game, poor boy,
   Deal John Hardy in the game."

3 John Hardy threw down a dollar on the board,
   Saying, "This is what I play,
   And the man who takes my money this time,
   I'm going to blow his life away, poor boy,
   I'm going to blow his life away."

4 John Hardy went away that night,
Expecting to be free;
A policeman took him by the arm,
Saying, "Won't you come and go with me, poor boy,
Won't you come and go with me?"

5 "Oh, I've been to the east and I've been to the west,
And I've traveled this wide world around,
Oh, I've been to the river and been baptized,
And now I'm on the hanging ground, good Lord!
And now I'm on the hanging ground.

THE WRECK ON THE C. & O.

This ballad originated in West Virginia. I remember hearing it sung by the "county fair singer" at the Gilmer County Fair, which was one of the big events of the year when I was a boy. The wreck on the C. & O. Railroad, in which George Alley was killed, occurred on October 23, 1890. The F. F. V. means "The Fast Flying Vestibule." For a complete account of the wreck, see Folk Songs of the South, *p. 211. Sung by John Breden, Nicholas County.*

A - long came the F. F. V., The fast-est on the line, Came run-ning in - to Hin - ton, Late be-hind the time.

2 When she blew for Hinton,
   The engineer was there;
   George Alley was his name,
   With bright and golden hair.

3 George's mother came to him
   With a basket on her arm,
   Says, "George, be careful how you run,
   Or you will come to harm.

4 "Many a man has lost his life
   From making up lost time;
   But if you'll run your engine right,
   You'll seldom be behind."

5 "Mother, I know your warning's true;
   But if I only had a local freight,
   I'd run her to Clifton Forge on time,
   Or drop her into hell."

6 He stepped into the cabin,
   There was his pal Jack;
   He looked over his engine,
   And looked along the track.

7 In the cabin they did ride.
   Says George, "A little extra steam,
   I mean to pull old Number 4
   The fastest ever seen.

8 "I mean to pull old Number 4
   With nerve known to all,
   And when I blow for the Big Bend Tunnel
   They'll only hear my call.

9 "I'll run her into Clifton Forge
   Or drop her into hell;
   Many a man has lost his life
   Working on the railroad.

10 "We've gone over these roads many a time,
   We know them all so well;
   I'll drop her into Clifton Forge
   Or sink her into hell.

11 "Look! Look! Jack!
   A rock ahead I see;
   I know there death is waiting
   To grab both you and me.

12 So from this cabin you must fly,
   I'll die for both you and me."
   "Oh, no, George, as to that,
   You and I cannot agree."

13 "But from this cabin you must fly,
   Your darling life to save;
   I want you to be an engineer
   When I am in my grave."

14 Just then she made a fatal dash,
   Upside down the engine crashed,
   The firebox open flew,
   And poor George's breast was smashed.

THE ORPHAN GIRL

This song used to bring tears when my Grandfather Gainer sang it to me when I was a little boy.

"No home, no home," cried the or-phan girl, At the door of the prince's___ hall, As she trem-bling stood on the pol-ished steps, And leaned on the pol-ished___ walls.

2 Her clothes were thin and her feet were bare,
   And the snow had covered her head.
   "Who'll give me a home?" she feebly said,
   "A home and a crust of bread?"

3 "My father, alas! I never knew,"
   With tears in her eyes so bright;
   "My mother sleeps in her new-made grave,
   "Tis an orphan that begs tonight.

4 "I'll freeze," she said as she sank on the steps
   And strove to cover her feet,
   With her tattered dress all covered with snow,
   All covered with snow and sleet.

5 The rich man lay on his velvet couch,
   And dreamed of his silver and gold,
   While the orphan lay on her bed of snow,
   And murmured, "So cold! So cold!"

6 The hours passed by and the midnight came,
  Rang out like a funeral knell;
  The earth was wrapped in a wintry sheet,
  And the drift of the snow still fell.

7 The morning came, but the orphan girl
  Still lay at the rich man's door,
  But her soul had fled to a home in heaven,
  Where there's room and there's bread for the poor.

THE·REJECTED LOVER

I have heard Grandfather Gainer say that when he went back to Barbour County to see his relatives, people asked him to sing this song when he stopped to stay all night. He was an excellent singer.

Oh, once I had a pret-ty girl, And I loved her as my life, And I'd free-ly give my heart and hand To make her my wife. Oh, ____ to make her my wife.

2 She took me by the hand,
  And she led me to the door,
  And she put her arms around me
  Saying, "You can't come any more,
  Oh, you can't come any more."

3 But I'd not been gone but six weeks,
  Before she did complain,
  And she wrote to me a letter
  Saying, "O do come again,
  O do come again."

4 But I wrote to her an answer,
  Just for to let her know
  That no young man would venture
  Where he once could not go,
  Oh, he once could not go.

5 Come all you true lovers,
  Take warning by me,
  And never leave your affections
  On a green growing tree,
  Oh, a green growing tree.

6 For the leaves they will wither,
  And the roots they will decay;
  And the beauty of a fair maid
  Will soon fade away.
  Oh, will soon fade away.

ONE MORNING IN MAY

The lady who sang this song, Lenore Danley, of Gilmer County, said she had heard it called "The Nightingale Song," but always called it "One Morning in May." The delightful tune adds much to the charm of this little ballad.

One morn-ing, one morn-ing, one morn-ing in May, I saw a young cou - ple a walk-ing their way. One was a maid-en so slim and so fair, The oth - er was a sol-dier, a brave vol-un - teer.

2 "Good morning, good morning, good morning to thee,
Oh, where are you going, my pretty lady?"
"I'm going a walking, because it is spring,
To see the waters gliding, hear the nightingale sing."

3 They had not been standing but a moment or two,
When out from his knapsack a fiddle he drew,
And the tunes that he played to her made the hills ring,
'Twas prettier than the music when the nightingales sing.

4 "O pretty fair lady, it's time to give o'er."
"No, no, pretty soldier, play just one tune more.
I rather would listen to the sound of your string,
Than see the waters gliding, hear the nightingales sing.

5 "Pretty soldier, pretty soldier, will you marry me?"
"Oh, no, pretty lady, that can never be,
For I have a wife and children twice three.
Two wives are too many, too many for me.

6 "And now, pretty lady, I'm going away,
   But I'll always remember this morning in May.
   If I ever return it will be in the spring,
   To see the waters glide, hear the nightingale sing."

THE PRETTY MOHEA

This song has often appeared in print, sometimes under the titles, "The Pretty Maumee," or "The Little Maumee." Sung by Eugene Robinson, Nicholas County.

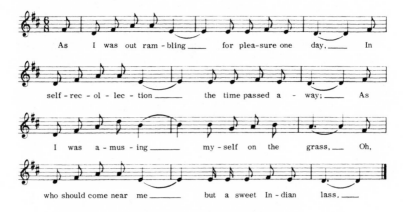

As I was out ram-bling_____ for plea-sure one day,_____ In self-rec-ol-lec-tion_____ the time passed a - way;_____ As I was a-mus-ing_____ my-self on the grass,_____ Oh, who should come near me_____ but a sweet In-dian lass._____

2 She sat down beside me and gave me her hand,
  Saying, "You look like a stranger, not one of this land."
  Saying, "If you are willing, you're welcome to come
  And live in a cottage that I call my home."

3 "Oh no, my fair maiden, that could never be,
  For I have a sweetheart far over the sea;
  I'll never forsake her, for I know she won't me,
  For her heart is as true as the Pretty Mohea."

4 So one fair May morning, one morning in May,
  To this fair Indian maiden these words I did say:
  "I'm going to leave you, so farewell, my dear,
  My ships are now sailing, and home I must steer."

5 The last time I saw her was down on the strand,
As my boat passed by her she waved me her hand,
Saying, "When you get home, dear, far over the sea,
Remember the maiden call Pretty Mohea."

6 And now I have landed on my native shore,
With friends and relations around me once more;
Of all that's around me there's none that I see,
That is fit to compare with the Pretty Mohea.

ON ERIN'S GREEN SHORE

This song is sometimes called "The Irishman's Dream." It appeared in numerous English broadsides. The young man who is sleeping on Erin's green shore is awakened from sleep by the spirit of his sister, who has come from England to prevent his capture by the British soldiers. When he awakens, the vision of his sister disappears. Sung by Mary Bell Workman.

One eve - ning for plea-sure I ram - bled Down by a clear pour - ing stream,___ I sat down by a bed of prim - ros - es, And gent - ly fell in - to a dream.

2 I dreamt I saw a pretty fair damsel,
   Her equal I ne'er saw before;
   Her beauty there is none to compare with,
   As she strolled along on Erin's green shore.

3 She was dressed in the richest apparel,
   Green was the mantle she wore,
   All bound round with shamrock and roses,
   As she strolled along on Erin's green shore.

4 Her cheeks were like two full blooming roses,
   Her teeth were ivory white,
   Her eyes shone like two sparkling diamonds,
   Or the stars on some cold frosty night.

5 Quickly I addressed this fair maiden,
   "Fair jewel, pray tell me your name,
   I know you are a stranger in this country,
   Or you would not have acted so strange."

6 "I'm the daughter of Daniel O'Connor,
   From England I've lately come o'er,
   I've come here to awaken my brother
   Who slumbers on Erin's green shore."

7 In a transport of joy I awakened,
   To find it was only a dream.
   May the angels in heaven be her guardian,
   For I never shall see her again.

THE FAIR MAID IN THE GARDEN

This is one of several songs in which a lover returns from a long absence, but is not recognized by his true-love. He tests her love, and when he is assured that she still loves him, he shows her the gold ring that she had given him. When she sees the ring she recognizes her lover and falls at his feet. He gathers her in his arms and gives her kisses one, two, three. Sung by "Aunt" Mattie Long.

A fair maid stood in her fa-ther's gar-den;
Pluck-ing ros-es all cov-ered with dew; A strang-er came and gazed up-on her. Say-ing, "Pret-ty fair miss, will you mar-ry me?"

2 "I have a true-love in the army,
   And he's been gone for three long years,
   But if he's gone for three years longer,
   No man on earth will marry me."

3 "Perhaps your true-love he is wounded,
   Perhaps he's on some battlefield slain,
   Or perhaps he's to some other girl married,
   And you will ne'er see him again."

4 "Oh, if he's wounded I hope he's happy,
   Or if he's dead I wish him rest,
   But if he's to some other girl married,
   I'll love the one who married him."

5 He took his hand from out his pocket,
   His fingers being neat and trim,
   And on his finger he had a gold ring,
   As soon as she saw it at his feet she fell.

6 He gathered her up all in his arms,
   And kisses gave her one, two, three,
   Saying, "I'm your true and loving soldier,
   Just come back home for to wed with thee."

THE VILLAGE CHURCHYARD

This sentimental old song has brought tears to many singers and listeners through the years. Many a home had a special room called "the parlor," where the parlor organ was kept. The family often gathered around the organ, especially on Sunday, and sang hymns and songs like "The Village Churchyard." I have heard Aunt Mary Gainer Wilson sing this song many times in her fine soprano voice.

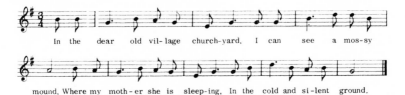

In the dear old vil-lage church-yard, I can see a mos-sy mound, Where my moth-er she is sleep-ing, In the cold and si-lent ground.

2 I was young but I remember
   Well the night my mother died;
   I stood there and nearly fainted,
   Till she called me to her side.

3 Saying, "Darling, I must leave you,
   Angel voices call me on,
   Pray that we may meet in heaven,
   When your mother's dead and gone."

4 Sweetly grows the weeping willow,
   Little birds to sing at dawn,
   I have no one left to love me
   Since my mother's dead and gone.

A LOVER'S LAMENT

A lamenting lover who sees the reflection of his grief in nature is an example of the "pathetic fallacy" in folk song. Aunt Mary Wilson, in another version of this song, sang: "Don't you see that little berry red, how it hangs on yander's vine? It's mourning in nature for its true love, just like I mourn for mine." I have found four versions of this song. This one was sung by Mr. W. A. Thomas.

I went a-bout from door to door, And what did I see but a lit-tle tur-tle dove, A - sit-ting on a ver-y tall pine, A - mourn-ing the loss of his own true love.

2 "O fare you well, my own true-love,
  For I must leave you for a while,
  And never more will I return
  Till I have gone ten thousand miles.

3 "O who will shoe your bonny feet,
  And who will glove your little hands,
  And who will kiss your ruby lips
  When I am gone to a foreign land?"

4 "My father will shoe my bonny feet,
  My mother will glove my little hands,
  And you may kiss these ruby lips
  When you return from the foreign land."

5 O don't you see that lonesome dove,
  As it flies about from pine to pine?
  It's mournin' for its own true-love,
  Just like I would mourn for mine.

MARY OF THE WILD MOOR

Many people have asked for this song. It has appeared in print many times, both in the British Isles and in America. It was sung by Mrs. R. R. Umbarger, Nicholas County.

It was all on a cold win-ter's night, When the wind blew a-cross the wild moor, When Ma-ry came wan-der-ing home with her child, Till she came to her own fa-ther's door.

2 "Oh, please, father come down to me now,
   Do come down, please, and open the door,
   For the child in my arms will perish and die
   From the winds that blow 'cross the wild moor."

3 But the old man was deaf to her cries,
   Not a sound of her voice did he hear,
   But the watchdog did howl and the bell tolled the hour,
   And the winds blew across the wild moor.

4 Oh how sad the old man must have felt
   When he came to the door in the morn,
   And found Mary dead, but the child was alive,
   Tightly clasped in his dead mother's arms.

5 And with anguish he tore his gray hair,
   While the tears down his cheeks they did roll,
   Saying, "There Mary died, once the gay village bride,
   From the winds that blew 'cross the wild moor."

6 Then with sorrow the old man soon died,
  And the child to his mother went soon;
  There is no one, they say, has lived there to this day,
  And the cottage to ruin has gone.

7 Now the villagers oft point to the spot
  Where the willows droop over the door,
  Saying, "There Mary died, once the gay village bride,
  From the winds that blew 'cross the wild moor."

O FATHER, BUILD ME A BOAT

This song has long been popular in West Virginia. It was sung to me by my great-aunt Mary Wilson, whose great-great-grandfather came from Ireland in 1725. I also heard the song in Ireland when I was recording folk songs there in 1961.

It was ear - ly, ear - ly in the month of May, Down by the green fields I chanced to stray; __ I heard a fe - male __ to sigh and say, The lad she loved __ was gone far a - way.

2 "O, father, father, build me a boat,
For o'er the ocean I long to float,
To watch the big ships as they pass by,
And to enquire of my sailor boy."

3 She was not long floating on the deep,
When three large vessels she chanced to meet,
Saying, "Captain, Captain, come tell me true,
Is my love Willie on board with you?"

4 "What color clothes did your Willie wear?
What color was your true love's hair?"
"His hair was black and his eyes were blue,
And he wore a coat of the navy blue."

5 "Oh, no, oh no, he is not here,
For he is drowned I greatly fear;
It was at Green Island as we passed by,
We lost three more and your sailor boy."

6 She wrung her hands and she tore her hair
   Like any fair maid in deep despair;
   She dashed her small boat against the rocks,
   Saying, "What shall I do, now my love is lost?

7 "Now I'll sit down and I'll write a song,
   And if I write it I'll write it long;
   For every line I'll shed a tear,
   And for every verse I'll cry, 'Willie, dear.'

8 "Oh, dig my grave and dig it deep,
   Put a marble stone at my head and feet;
   And in the middle put a turtle dove,
   To let the world know that I died for love."

FAIR CHARLOTTE

This song, which is thoroughly broadside in style, became very popular all over the United States in the latter part of the nineteenth century. Although it is a tragedy and supposed to cause tears, young people today usually think it ridiculously funny. One young man remarked: "How could Charles be so dumb as to let the girl freeze to death sitting by him in the sleigh, and not put his arms around her until after she was dead?" It is probably no more ridiculous than some of the modern "country songs"—such as "I Lie In My Bed On My Back With My Ears Full of Tears Over You." Sung by Helen Blankenship, Nicholas County.

Fair Charlotte lived on a mountain side, In a wild and lonely spot; There was no dwelling for five miles around, Except her father's cot.

2 One New Year's eve, as the sun went down,
   Far looked her wishful eye,
   One from the frosty window pane,
   As the merry sleighs dashed by.

3 At the village, fifteen miles away,
   Was to be a ball that night,
   And though the air was piercing cold,
   Her heart was warm and light.

4 How brightly beamed her laughing eye
   As a well-known voice she heard,
   And dashing up to the cottage door,
   Her lover's sleigh appeared.

5 "O daughter," the mother cried,
  "This blanket round you fold:
  For 'tis a dreadful night abroad,
  And you will get your death of cold."

6 "O nay, O nay!" fair Charlotte cried,
  As she laughed like a gypsy queen;
  "To ride in a blanket muffled up
  I never would be seen.

7 "My silken cloak is quite enough,
  You know 'tis lined throughout;
  And there is my silken scarf to twine
  My head and neck about."

8 Her bonnet and her gloves were on,
  She jumped into the sleigh,
  And swiftly they sped down the mountain side
  And o'er the hills away.

9 With muffled beat so silently
  Five miles at last were passed,
  When Charles with few and shivering words
  The silence broke at last.

10 "Such a dreadful night I never saw,
  My reins I scarce can hold."
  Fair Charlotte very faintly replied,
  "I am exceeding cold."

11 He cracked his whip and urged his steed
  Much faster than before,
  And thus five other dreary miles
  In silence were passed o'er.

12 Spoke Charles, "How fast the freezing ice
  Is gathering on my brow!"
  And Charlotte still more faintly said,
  "I'm growing warmer now."

13 Thus on they rode through the frosty air
  And the glittering, cold starlight,
  Until at last the village lamps
  And the ballroom came in sight.

14 They reached the door and Charles sprang out,
   And held his hand to her;
   "Why sit you like a monument
   That hath no power to stir?"

15 He called her once and called her twice,
   She answered not a word;
   He asked her for her hand again,
   But still she never stirred.

16 And then he took her hand in his,
   'Twas cold and hard as stone;
   He tore the mantle from her face,
   And the cold stars o'er it shone.

17 Then quickly to the lighted hall
   Her lifeless form he bore;
   Fair Charlotte's eyes had closed for aye,
   And her voice was heard no more.

18 And there he sat down by her side,
   While bitter tears did flow,
   And cried, "My own, my charming bride,
   You never more shall know!"

19 He twined his arms around her neck
   And kissed her marble brow,
   And his thoughts flew back to where she said,
   "I'm growing warmer now."

THE WEALTHY SQUIRE

*This song, of English origin, was printed in this country as a broad-
side early in the nineteenth century. Many American texts have been
printed, and Professor Cox found five variants in West Virginia. In folk
tales and songs women often resort to some kind of trickery to get the
man they love. In this cunning little story in song the lady falls in love
with a farmer, disguises herself as a young man with dog and gun,
purposely loses her glove so that the farmer will find it and claim the
reward, which is the lady herself. Sung by Mr. H. B. Bryant.*

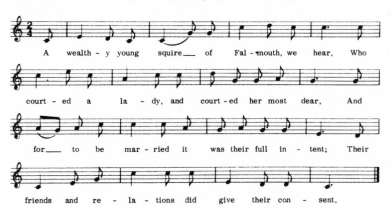

A wealth-y young squire___ of Fal-mouth, we hear, Who
court-ed a la-dy, and court-ed her most dear, And
for___ to be mar-ried it was their full in-tent; Their
friends and re-la-tions did give their con-sent.

2 The time was appointed for the wedding day,
The farmer was appointed to give her away;
When the handsome farmer the lady did spy,
Her heart was inflamed. "Oh, my heart!" she did cry.

3 She turned herself around, though nothing she said,
Instead of being married, she took to her bed;
The thought of the farmer still running in her mind,
And a way for to win him she quickly did find.

4 Vest, coat, and breeches this lady put on,
   Then away she went a-hunting with her dog and her gun;
   She hunted all around where this farmer used to dwell,
   Because in her heart she did love him so well.

5 Full many times she fired, though nothing she killed,
   Until this handsome farmer came into the field,
   And for a little discourse she quickly begun,
   As she was a-hunting with her dog and gun.

6 "O why do you not go to the wedding?" she cried,
   To wait upon the squire and to give him his bride?"
   "Oh no," said the farmer, "If the truth I must tell,
   I'll not give her away, for I love her so well."

7 The lady was pleased to hear him so bold,
   She handed him a glove all bordered with gold;
   She told him she had found it just as she came along,
   As she was a-hunting with her dog and her gun.

8 Then she gave out the news that she had lost her glove,
   And the man that would find it she'd grant him her love;
   "The man that will find it and bring it to me,
   The man that will find it, his bride I will be."

9 The farmer was pleased to hear what she did say,
   And straightway to the lady made his way,
   Saying, "Honored lady, I have picked up your glove,
   And now will you please to grant me your love?"

10 "It is already granted," the lady replied,
    I'll dearly love the breath of the farmer," she cried;
    "I'll be mistress of my dairy, go milking the cows,
    While my jolly farmer goes whistling to his plow."

11 But after the wedding she told of her fun,
    How she went a-hunting with her dog and her gun,
    Saying, "Now that I have got him all safe in my snare,
    I'll love him forever, I do vow and declare."

COME ALL YOU FAIR AND TENDER LADIES

This song was one of my Grandfather Gainer's favorites. It is printed here as I learned it from him.

Come, all you fair and ___ ten - der ___ la - dies, Be care - ful how you ___ court young ___ men; They're like a star on a fair sum-mer's morn-ing, They first ap -pear and ___ then they're gone.

2 They'll tell to you some flattering story,
   And then declare they love you well,
   And away they'll go and court some other,
   And leave you here in grief to dwell.

3 I wish to the Lord I had never seen him,
   Or in his cradle he had died;
   To think a fair and tender lady,
   Did fall in love and was denied.

4 I wish I was a little sparrow,
   And one of them that could fly so high;
   I would fly away to my true love's dwelling,
   When he would speak I'd be close by.

5 But I am none of those little sparrows,
   Or none of those that fly so high,
   So I'll sit down in grief and sorrow,
   And hope my morrow will pass by.

6 O, love is handsome, love is charming,
   And love is beauty while it's new;
   But love grows older, love grows colder,
   It fades away like the morning dew.

I WISH I WAS SINGLE AGAIN

The minstrel songs of the Old World were not brought to America, for they were not as a rule sung in the home but by professional minstrels—who did not come to America. But in time there did develop in America a kind of singing comparable to that of the Old World minstrel. The American singer entertained the people at the county fair or on the courthouse square in the village, singing stories of disasters in America, such as floods, fires, railroad wrecks, the exploits of heroes and bad men, and always with a good store of humorous songs. He usually accompanied his singing with a banjo. This song was one of the most popular in his repertoire. I heard it as a boy at a county fair.

Oh I wish I was sin - gle a - gain, _____ I wish I was sin-gle a - gain, _____ When I was sin -gle, the mon - ey did jin-gle, So I wish I was sin - gle a - gain. _____

2 I married me a wife, oh then,
   I married me a wife, oh then,
   I married me a wife, she's ruined my life,
     So I wish I was single again.

3 She binged me, she banged me, oh then,
   She binged me, she banged me, oh then,
   She binged me, she banged me, she thought she would hang me,
     Oh I wish I was single again.

4 She went for the rope, oh then,
   She went for the rope, oh then,
   She went for the rope, when she got there 'twas broke,
     Oh I wish I was single again.

5 My wife she died, oh then,
　My wife she died, oh then,
　My wife she died, I laughed till I cried,
　　To think I was single again.

6 I went to the funeral, oh then,
　I went to the funeral, oh then,
　I went to the funeral and danced Yankee Doodle
　　To think I was single again.

7 I married me another, oh then,
　I married me another, oh then,
　I married me another, she was, worse than the tother,
　　Oh I wish I was single again.

8 Yes, I married me another, oh then,
　I married me another, oh then,
　I married me another, she's the devil's grandmother,
　　Oh I wish I was single again.

WILL THÈ WEAVER

This humorous song was sung by Jim Fluharty, of Wirt County. There are several ballads which tell how a husband, suspecting his wife's unfaithfulness, returns unexpectedly and discovers his wife's lover. In one ballad the lover hides in a chest; the husband carries it out of the house, then opens it and gives his rival a kick in the rear. In this story, Will the weaver hides in the chimney and is smoked out when the husband builds a fire. The last line of verse 13 is an excellent example of folk humor: "Come here no more to stop my smoke."

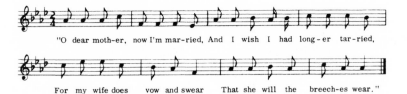

"O dear mother, now I'm married, And I wish I had longer tarried,
For my wife does vow and swear That she will the breeches wear."

2 "O dear son, go home and hug her,
And no more of her faults discover,
But when she does at all rebel,
Just pull a sprout and switch her well."

3 As he went home a neighbor met him,
And told him something for to fret him,
"Neighbor, neighbor, I tell you how,
What I saw at your home just now.

4 "There I saw that Will the Weaver
And your wife stand close together
On the steps ferninst the door;
They went in, I saw no more."

5 He went home like one in wonder,
On the door he knocked like thunder.
"Who comes there?" the weaver cried.
"It's my husband, you must hide."

146

6 Then the door she opened wide,
And her husband stepped inside.
She began to make a moan,
"I'm by myself and all alone.

7 "You go out to seek your pleasure,
Spending all your golden treasure,
Leaving me, poor wife, at home,
All alone to make my moan."

8 "O my wife, be not in rage,
I'd have you do as I engage,
Draw some cider, for I am dry."
Like a good wife she did comply.

9 While she was gone he did endeavor
For to search out this Will the Weaver;
He searched the room around and around,
But not a soul could there be found.

10 He stood on the hearth as one amazed,
And up the chimney as he gazed,
He there spied out that wretched soul
Sitting astride the chimney pole.

11 "Ho, ho!" snorts he, "and now I've found you,
I will neither hang nor drown you,
But I will cover you with smoke."
So he thought, but little spoke.

12 Then he built a roaring fire,
Much against his wife's desire,
She cried out, "As I'm your wife,
Take him down and spare his life."

13 So off the chimney pole he took him,
And so merrily he shook him,
Shouting out at every stroke,
"Come here no more to stop my smoke."

14 Was ever any chimney sweeper
Half so black as Will the Weaver?
With hands and clothes and sooty face
He sent him home in this disgrace.

A BLIND MAN HE CAN SEE

This humorous ballad is of Old World origin. It was sung to me by my grandfather Gainer, whose great-great-grandfather came from Ireland.

There was a wise old wom-an, and her sto-ry I will tell, She loved her hus-band dear-ly and an-oth-er man twice as well, With a ti-ga-ree to-rum o-rum, And a blind man he can see.

2 Now she went to the doctor and told to him her mind,
"Please give me some medicine to make my husband blind."
    With a tigaree torum orum,
    And a blind man he can see.

3 "Go get some eggs and marrow bones and make him suck them all,
And I know that in a very short time he can't see you at all."
    With a tigaree torum orum,
    And a blind man he can see.

4 The doctor sent for this old man and told what she had spoke,
The old man thanked the doctor then and said he'd play the joke.
    With a tigaree torum orum,
    And a blind man he can see.

5 She got some eggs and marrow bones and made him suck them all,
And he cried, "My dearest wife, I can't see you at all."
    With a tigaree torum orum,
    And a blind man he can see.

6 "In this world I have no pleasure, Oh, I do not wish to stay,
I would go today and drown myself if I could find the way."
With a tigaree torum orum,
And a blind man he can see.

7 "O my dear, if you would drown yourself, and do not wish to stay,
Then let me take your hand, my dear, and I will show the way."
With a tigaree torum orum,
And a blind man he can see.

8 "Now I'll stand on the river bank while you run up the hill,
Then push me in with all your might." "My dear," she said, "I will."
With a tigaree torum orum,
And a blind man he can see.

9 And when she ran with all her might to push her husband in,
All he did was step aside, and headlong she went in.
With a tigaree torum orum,
And a blind man he can see.

10 She cried, "My dearest husband, please don't leave me here behind."
He said, "I can't help you, my wife, because you know I'm blind."
With a tigaree torum orum,
And a blind man he can see.

WHERE ARE YOU GOING, MY PRETTY FAIR MAID?

This song was sung to me by my Aunt Mary Wilson, my grand-father's sister. Although the song has appeared in numerous books in America, Aunt Mary did not get it from a book, for she had never learned to read. She learned it when she was a girl, but she did not remember where.

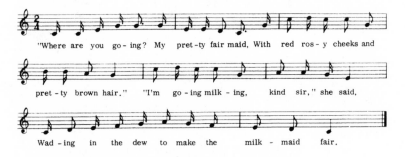

"Where are you go-ing? My pret-ty fair maid, With red ros-y cheeks and pret-ty brown hair." "I'm go-ing milk-ing, kind sir," she said, Wad-ing in the dew to make the milk-maid fair.

    2 "Who is your father? My pretty fair maid,
        With red rosy cheeks and pretty brown hair?"
        "My father's a farmer, kind sir," she said.
        Wading in the dew to make the milkmaid fair.

    3 "Who is your mother? My pretty fair maid,
        With red rosy cheeks and pretty brown hair?"
        "My mother's a weaver, kind sir," she said.
        Wading in the dew to make the milkmaid fair.

    4 "What is your fortune? My pretty fair maid,
        With red rosy cheeks and pretty brown hair."
        "My face is my fortune, kind sir," she said.
        Wading in the dew to make the milkmaid fair.

    5 "Then I'll not marry you, my pretty fair maid,
        With red rosy cheeks and pretty brown hair."
        "Nobody asked you to, kind sir," she said,
        Wading in the dew to make the milkmaid fair.

ST. CLAIR'S DEFEAT

This American historical ballad describes the defeat of the United States army under the command of General Arthur St. Clair in a battle against the Miami Indians in 1791. St. Clair was a Scottish-American soldier and statesman, who became an officer in the British army and served in America during the French and Indian War. He resigned from the army in 1762 and settled on an estate in western Pennsylvania. When the Revolutionary War broke out, he joined the Colonial army and organized the New Jersey troops.

After the war St. Clair became interested in politics and was elected to the Continental Congress. In 1787 he became president of the Congress, and in 1789 was made governor of the Northwest Territory. Two years later he was given command of the United States army and fought the disastrous battle against the Indians.

The origin of the ballad is unknown, and we have found but one version of it in West Virginia which was sung to me by Mr. W. A. Thomas.

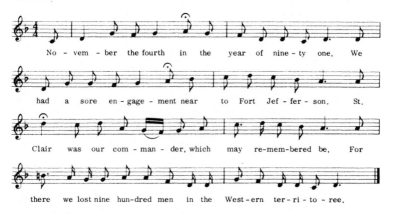

No - vem - ber the fourth in the year of nine - ty one, We had a sore en - gage - ment near to Fort Jef - fer - son. St. Clair was our com - man - der, which may re - mem-bered be, For there we lost nine hun-dred men in the West - ern ter - ri - to - ree.

2 Our army was attacked just as the day did dawn,
  And soon were overpowered and driven from the lawn.
  They killed Major Oldham, Levine and Briggs likewise,
  While horrid yells of savages resounded through the skies.

3 We charged with courage firm, but soon again gave ground.
The warwhoop then redoubled, as did the foes around.
They killed Major Ferguson, which caused the men to cry,
"Our only safety is in flight or fighting here to die."

4 Yet three hours more we fought them, but soon were forced to yield.
When three hundred bloody warriors were stretched upon the field.
Said Colonel Gibson to his men, "My boys, be not dismayed,
I'm sure that true Virginians were never yet afraid."

5 Alas, the dying and wounded, how dreadful was the thought,
To the tomahawk and scalping knife in misery were brought.
Some had a thigh and some an arm broke in this dire affray,
To die in torment at the stake to close the awful day.

BROTHER GREEN

There were many songs that came out of Civil War experiences.
Most of these are sentimental, such as "Just Before the Battle, Mother,"
"Tenting On the Old Camp Ground," and "Brother Green." These
songs first appeared as broadsides, then passed into oral tradition and
became folk songs. Sung by Mr. M. W. McCourt, Webster County.

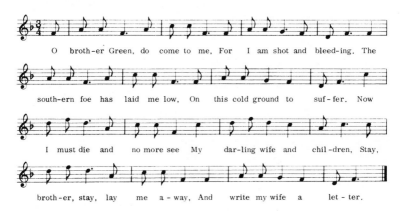

O broth-er Green, do come to me, For I am shot and bleed-ing. The
south-ern foe has laid me low, On this cold ground to suf-fer. Now
I must die and no more see My dar-ling wife and chil-dren, Stay,
broth-er, stay, lay me a-way, And write my wife a let-ter.

2 Tell her I am prepared to go,
  I hope we'll meet in heaven.
  When I believed in Jesus Christ,
  My sins were all forgiven.

  I know that she has prayed for me,
  I know her prayers were answered,
  That I would be prepared to die
  If I should fall in battle.

3 My little babes, I love them well,
  Oh, could I once more see them,
  To bid them all a long farewell
  Till we do meet in heaven.

But here I am in Tennessee,
And they are in Ohio,
Too far away from them I know,
To hear their silvery voices.

4 Dear Mary, you must use them well,
And teach them up for Jesus;
Teach them to love and serve the Lord,
And they will be respected.

O sister Anna, do not weep
For the loss of your dear brother,
For I'm to dwell with Jesus Christ,
And see my blessed mother.

5 Go tell my wife she must not weep,
Go kiss my tender children.
I know they'll call for me in vain
When I am up in heaven

Two brothers yet I can't forget,
They're fighting for the Union,
For which, dear wife, I've lost my life
To put down this rebellion.

6 O brother Green, I'm dying now,
Oh, but I die so easy;
I know that death has lost its sting,
Because I love my Jesus.

O father, you have suffered long,
And prayed for my salvation,
Now I must die and leave you all,
So fare you well, temptation.

THE DRUMMER BOY OF WATERLOO

This well-known English broadside may have come to America in print, and then became traditional, or it may have come in oral tradition directly from England. A version of it appeared in The American Songster *(Philadelphia, 1850), and another version appeared in* Folk Songs of the South, 1925. *This version from Ritchie County was contributed by Dewey Wass of Harrisville.*

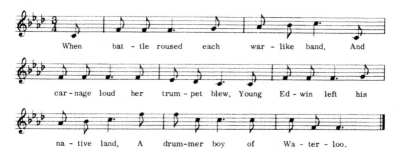

When bat - tle roused each war - like band, And car - nage loud her trum - pet blew, Young Ed - win left his na - tive land, A drum-mer boy of Wa - ter - loo.

2 His mother when his lips she pressed,
   And bade her noble son adieu,
   With wringing hands, with aching heart,
   Beheld him march for Waterloo.

3 But he who knew no infant fears
   His knapsack o'er his shoulder threw,
   And cried, "Dear mother, dry those tears
   Till I return from Waterloo."

4 He went, but ere the set of sun,
   Before our arms the foe subdue,
   The flash of death that murderous gun
   Had laid him low at Waterloo.

5 "O comrades, comrades," Edwin cried,
   And proudly beamed his eyes of blue,
   "Go tell my mother Edwin died
   A soldier's death at Waterloo."

6 They placed his head upon his drum,
   Beneath the moon's pale mournful hue.
   When night had stilled the battle's hum
   They dug his grave at Waterloo.

SOLDIER, WILL YOU MARRY ME?

This song used to delight us as children when Grandfather sang it. Cox prints a version of it which was obtained from William Gainer, my grandfather's brother. Each time it was sung it was likely to be varied so that the soldier got a complete outfit of clothing before he revealed that he was already married.

"Sol - dier, sol - dier, will you mar - ry me, With your mus - ket, fife and drum?" "Oh, how can I mar - ry such a pret - ty lit - tle girl, When I have no suit to put on?"

2 Away she ran to the tailor's shop
   As fast as she could run,
   She got a suit, a very fine suit,
   And the soldier put it on.

3 "Soldier, soldier, will you marry me,
   With your musket, fife, and drum?"
   "Oh, how can I marry such a pretty little girl,
   When I have no shoes to put on?"

4 Away she ran to the cobbler's shop,
   As fast as she could run,
   She got some shoes, some very fine shoes,
   And the soldier put them on.

5 "Soldier, soldier, will you marry me,
   With your musket, fife, and drum?"
   "Oh, how can I marry such a pretty little girl,
   When I have no hat to put on?"

6 Away she ran to the hatter's shop,
   As fast as she could run,
   She got a hat, a very fine hat,
   And the soldier put it on.

7 "Soldier, soldier, will you marry me,
   With your musket, fife, and drum?"
   "Oh, how can I marry such a pretty little girl,
   When I have a sweet wife at home?"

THE SOLDIER'S POOR LITTLE BOY

My grandfather learned this song when he was a boy at the time of the Civil War. I learned it from him when I was a small boy.

The snow was fast-ly fall-ing, The wind— did loud-ly roar, When a

poor lit-tle boy 'most fro - zen Came— up to a rich la-dy's door.

2 He spied her at the window high,
It filled his heart with joy,
Saying, "For mercy sake, some pity on me take.
I'm a soldier's poor little boy.

3 "My mother died when I was young,
My father's gone to the war,
And many a battle brave he's fought,
He's covered with wounds and with scars.

4 "And many a mile on his knapsack
He's carried me with joy,
But now I am left quite parentless,
I'm a soldier's poor little boy."

5 She then arose from the window so high,
And opened the door to him,
Saying, "Come in, come in, you poor little boy,
You never shall wander again.

6 "My own dear son in the battle was slain,
My own, my life, my joy;
So long as I live, some shelter I'll give
To a soldier's poor little boy."

THE OLD COUPLE AND THE PIG

This is strictly a children's song to be sung for the entertainment of small children. I knew it as a child and I heard it later from Pearl Bell.

There was an old coup-le who bought a lit-tle pig,— Huh, huh, huh. There was an old coup-le who bought a lit-tle pig, It did-n't cost much for it was-n't ver-y big.— Huh, huh, huh.

2 This little pig did lots of harm,
   Huh, huh, huh.
   This little pig did lots of harm,
   The plagued little thing ran all around the farm.
   Huh, huh, huh.

3 The little pig died for want of breath,
   Huh, huh, huh.
   The little pig died for want of breath,
   Wasn't that an awful death?
   Huh, huh, huh.

4 The old man died on account of grief,
   Huh, huh, huh.
   The old man died on account of grief,
   Wasn't that a great relief?
   Huh, huh, huh.

5 The old woman weeped and she moaned and she cried,
      Huh, huh, huh.
   The old woman weeped and she moaned and she cried,
   Then she lay right down and died.
      Huh, huh, huh.

6 There they lay all three on the shelf,
      Huh, huh, huh.
   There they lay all three on the shelf,
   If you want any more you can sing it yourself.
      Huh, huh, huh.

MR. FROG WENT A-COURTIN'

This Old World song has been very popular in West Virginia. Dr. Cox reported seven variants in Folk Songs of the South. *See his note for further information. Sung by Pearl Gould, Gilmer County.*

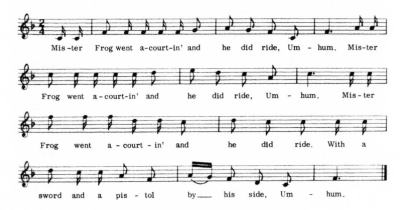

Mis-ter Frog went a-court-in' and he did ride, Um - hum. Mis-ter
Frog went a-court-in' and he did ride, Um - hum. Mis-ter
Frog went a - court - in' and he did ride. With a
sword and a pis - tol by — his side, Um - hum.

2 He rode right up to Miss Mousie's door, Um-hum.
He rode right up to Miss Mousie's door, Um-hum.
He rode right up to Miss Mousie's door,
Just like he had done before, Um-hum.

3 He rode right up to Miss Mousie's den, Um-hum.
He rode right up to Miss Mousie's den, Um-hum.
He rode right up to Miss Mousie's den,
He said, "Miss Mousie, are you within?" Um-hum

4 "O yes, kind sir, I am within," Um-hum.
"O yes, kind sir, I am within," Um-hum.
"O yes, kind sir, I am within,
Just lift the latch and walk right in." Um-hum.

5   He took Miss Mousie upon his knee, Um-hum.
    He took Miss Mousie upon his knee, Um-hum.
    He took Miss Mousie upon his knee,
    And said, "Miss Mousie, will you marry me?" Um-hum.

6   "O where shall the wedding supper be?" Um-hum.
    "O where shall the wedding supper be?" Um-hum.
    "O where shall the wedding supper be?"
    "Way down in the hollow of an old oak tree." Um-hum.

7   "What shall the wedding supper be?" Um-hum.
    "What shall the wedding supper be?" Um-hum.
    "What shall the wedding supper be?"
    "A big slice of cake and a cup of tea." Um-hum.

8   The first came in was a bumble bee, Um-hum.
    The first came in was a bumble bee, Um-hum.
    The first came in was a bumble bee,
    A-carryin' a fiddle upon his knee. Um-hum.

9   The next came in was a big black bug, Um-hum.
    The next came in was a big black bug, Um-hum.
    The next came in was a big black bug,
    And on his back was a whisky jug. Um-hum.

10 A sword and a pistol on the shelf, Um-hum.
    A sword and a pistol on the shelf, Um-hum.
    A sword and a pistol on the shelf,
    If you want any more you can sing it yourself. Um-hum.
    Um-hum

THE BARNYARD SONG

This song is intended for group singing by small children. It was sung by school children of Logan County in 1958.

1. I had a cat and my cat pleased me. I fed my cat un-der yon-der tree. Cat goes fid-dle-i - fee.

2. I had a hen and the hen pleased me. I fed my hen un-der yon-der tree. Hen goes chim-my chuck, chim-my chuck, cat goes fid-dle-i - fee.

3. I had a duck and the duck pleased me. I fed my duck un-der yon-der tree. Duck goes quack, quack, hen goes chim-my chuck, chim-my chuck, cat goes fid-dle-i - fee.

4 Goose . . . swish-y, swash-y . . .

5 Sheep . . . baa, baa . . .

6 Hog . . . grif-fy, gruf-fy . . .

7 Cow . . . moo, moo . . .

8 Horse . . . neigh, neigh . . .

9 Dog . . . bow, wow.

(Repeat all previous lines after each additional stanza)

BILLY BOY

This is the kind of song our great-grandmother used to sing for us children when she came to spend the night with us. We would gather around her and ask her to tell stories and sing songs. When we asked her to sing "Billy Boy" she would say, "All right, children, now you get out your slates and figure out how old the woman was that Billy Boy wanted for his wife. And the first one that gets it will get a prize." She always had a cookie or an apple in her apron pocket to give the one who first got the answer. But each time she sang the song she would change the numbers.

"O ____ where have you been, Bil - ly Boy, Bil - ly Boy, O ____ where have you been charm-ing Bil- ly?" "O I've been to seek a wife, she's the joy ___ of my life, But she's a young thing and can- not leave her mam-my."

2 "O did she ask you in, Billy Boy, Billy Boy?
   O did she ask you in, charming Billy?"
   "O yes, she asked me in, she has a dimple in her chin,
       But she's a young thing and cannot leave her mammy."

3 "Can she bake a cherry pie, Billy Boy, Billy Boy?
   Can she bake a cherry pie, charming Billy?"
   "She can bake a cherry pie quick as a cat can wink its eye,
       But she's a young thing and cannot leave her mammy."

4 "Can she bake a sweetened pone, Billy Boy, Billy Boy?
   Can she bake a sweetened pone, charming Billy?"
   "She can bake a sweetened pone, you can eat it or let it alone,
       But she's a young thing and cannot leave her mammy."

5 "Can she make a feather bed, Billy Boy, Billy Boy?
    Can she make a feather bed, charming Billy?"
"She can make a feather bed, put the pillers at the head,
    But she's a young thing and cannot leave her mammy."

6 "How tall is she, Billy Boy, Billy Boy?
    How tall is she, charming Billy?"
"She's as tall as a pine and straight as a punkin vine,
    But she's a young thing and cannot leave her mammy."

7 "How old is she, Billy Boy, Billy Boy?
    How old is she, charming Billy?"
"Twice six, twice seven, twice forty and eleven,
    But she's a young thing and cannot leave her mammy."

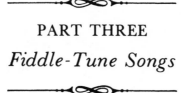

PART THREE
Fiddle-Tune Songs

The next seven songs in this book are fiddle-tune songs. The most popular instrument among mountain musicians is the fiddle. The word "fiddle" is of English origin, but the word "violin" for the same instrument is of Latin origin. Most of the old fiddle tunes popular among mountain fiddlers were brought to America just as the songs were brought—in oral tradition.

An older instrument, the rebec, of Arabic origin, was popular as a folk instrument in England as late as the seventeenth century. (See John Milton's poem, *L'Allegro.*) The rebec was an instrument with three strings, with one string fretted for the melody and the other two strings serving as drones. It was usually played with a bow or plucked with a quill. This instrument was also brought to America, but the fiddle with its four strings soon took first place as a folk instrument. The three-string instrument was revived in America around 1950 and now is being made and sold by scores of craftsmen. Today it is called the "plucked dulcimer," to distinguish it from the true dulcimer—which is now called the "hammered dulcimer."

Many of the old fiddle tunes had words and were often sung without the fiddle.

OLD JOE CLARK

The origins of the titles of many of the old fiddle tunes are very interesting, though many of them are hidden in the mystery of folklore. Some are named for unidentified persons, such as "Old Joe Clark," "Sally Goodin," "Cindy," and "Callaway." Some titles indicate place names, such as "Cumberland Gap," "Natchez on the Hill," and "Brushy Fork." Some are humorous, such as "Bile That Cabbage Down," "The Lop-Eared Mule," "Hell Up Coal Holler," "Granny, Will Your Dog Bite?" and "Hell Among the Yearlings." Some of the tunes are undoubtedly of Old World origin adapted to American historical events, such as "The Battle of Bull Run," and "Camp Chase." The tunes are always lively, and when there are words they are always humorous. Sung by Irene Murphy, Nicholas County.

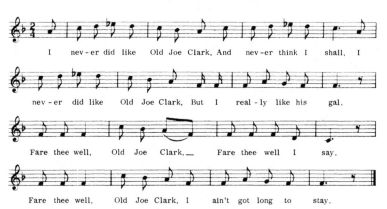

I never did like Old Joe Clark, And never think I shall, I never did like Old Joe Clark, But I really like his gal.

Fare thee well, Old Joe Clark, — Fare thee well I say.

Fare thee well, Old Joe Clark, I ain't got long to stay.

2   I never did like Old Joe Clark,
    And I'll tell you the reason why,
    He caught his heel in my rail fence
    And tore down all my rye.

    Fare thee well, Old Joe Clark,
    Fare thee well, I say.
    Fare thee well, Old Joe Clark,
    I ain't got long to stay.

171

3 The purtiest girl I ever saw
  Came running round the house,
  A yellow dog skin round her neck,
  The tail stuck in her mouth.

  Fare thee well, Old Joe Clark,
  Fare thee well, I say.
  Fare thee well, Old Joe Clark,
  I ain't got long to stay.

4 Old Joe Clark is a mean old man,
  And Old Joe Clark will steal,
  Old Joe Clark can go round the road,
  But he can't come through my field.

  Fare thee well, Old Joe Clark,
  Fare thee well, I say.
  Fare thee well, Old Joe Clark,
  I ain't got long to stay.

THE GIRL I LEFT BEHIND ME

This well-known song and fiddle tune has long been popular in Ireland. One young lady told me that her grandfather used to sing it to her when she was little, but when he came to the third stanza he couldn't remember the words and just sang, "Du duppa du duppa du." It is likely that her grandfather did remember the words but thought a little girl shouldn't hear them. I have transribed it here just as Granny sang it to me.

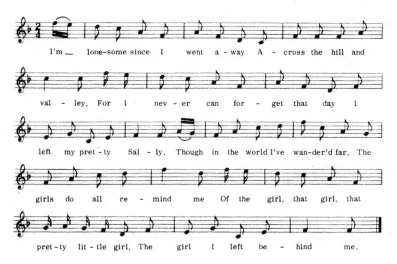

I'm lone-some since I went a-way A-cross the hill and val-ley, For I nev-er can for-get that day I left my pret-ty Sal-ly. Though in the world I've wan-der'd far, The girls do all re-mind me Of the girl, that girl, that pret-ty lit-tle girl, The girl I left be-hind me.

2 I never can forget the night
   When first she said she loved me,
   The stars peeped out and the moon shone bright
   On the girl I left behind me.

   But now I've gone to fight the foe,
   On the battlefield you'll find me,
   But I'll be going back to her,
   To the girl I left behind me.

173

3 She jumped in the bed and covered up her head,
   And said I could not find her.
   I raised up the sheet and she looked so neat,
   I jumped right in behind her.

   That girl, that girl, that pretty little girl,
   The girl I left behind me,
   She was pretty in the face and slim around the waist,
   The girl I left behind me.

SHADY GROVE

This is an old tune in the Dorian mode. The words do not give any clue as to the origin of the song. It is a very popular tune, no doubt of Old World origin. Sung by Andrew Burnside of Raleigh County.

Cheeks as red as the bloom-ing rose, Eyes of the deep-est brown, You are the dar - ling of my_heart, Stay till the sun goes down.

2 Shady Grove, my little love,
  Shady Grove, my dear,
  Shady Grove, my little love,
  I'm goin' to leave you here.

3 Shady Grove, my little love,
  Standin' in the door,
  Shoes and stockings in her hand,
  And her little bare feet on the floor.

4 Wish I had a big, fine horse,
  Corn to feed him on,
  Pretty little girl to stay at home,
  Feed him when I'm gone.

5 Shady Grove, my little love,
  Shady Grove, I say,
  Shady Grove, my little love,
  Don't wait till Judgment Day.

OLD DAN TUCKER

This is a good example of how a tune passes into tradition. Old Dan Tucker is a mythical old character who combed his hair with a wagon wheel and died with the toothache in his heel. The song was composed by Dan Emmett and became widely known through the old minstrel shows. My grandfather Gainer used to toss me on his knee and sing this song.

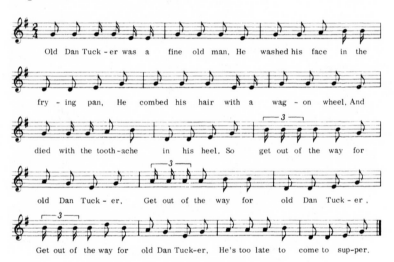

Old Dan Tuck-er was a fine old man, He washed his face in the fry-ing pan, He combed his hair with a wag-on wheel, And died with the tooth-ache in his heel. So get out of the way for old Dan Tuck-er, Get out of the way for old Dan Tuck-er, Get out of the way for old Dan Tuck-er, He's too late to come to sup-per.

2 Old Dan Tucker came to town
And drank a barrel of cider down;
The hoops flew off and the barrel burst,
And away went Dan in a thunder gust.

So get out of the way for Old Dan Tucker,
Get out of the way for old Dan Tucker,
Get out of the way for old Dan Tucker,
He's too late to come to supper.

3 Old Dan Tucker, he got drunk,
   He fell in the fire and kicked out a chunk,
   A red-hot coal got in his shoe,
   Lord a-mighty, how the ashes flew!

   So get out of the way for old Dan Tucker,
   Get out of the way for old Dan Tucker,
   Get out of the way for old Dan Tucker,
   He's too late to come to supper.

CINDY

This is a very popular song and fiddle tune. For songs of this kind, singers often made up extra verses as they sang. These words were then passed on to the next singer, and thus the song grew in tradition. This version was sung by Aunt Jennie Wilson, of Logan County.

I wish I was an ap - ple, A - hang - in' in the tree, And ev - 'ry time my Cin - dy passed, She'd take a bite of me. She told me that she loved me, She called me sug - ar plum, She throwed her arms a - round me and I thought my time had come. Get a - long home, Cin - dy, Cin - dy, Get a - long home, Cin - dy, Cin - dy, Get a - long home, Cin - dy, Cin - dy, I'll mar - ry you some time.

2 She took me to the parlor,
   She cooled me with her fan,
   She said I was the purtiest thing
   In the shape of mortal man.
   There's peaches in the summer
   And apples in the fall,
   But if I can't marry my Cindy girl,
   I won't get married at all.

Get along home, Cindy, Cindy,
Get along home, Cindy, Cindy,
Get along home, Cindy, Cindy,
I'll marry you some time.

3 Oh, Cindy got religion,
   She'd had it once before,
   But when she heard my old banjo
   She's the first one on the floor.
   I wish I had a needle,
   As fine as I could sew,
   I'd sew the girls to my coat tail
   And down the road I'd go.

   Get along home, Cindy, Cindy,
   Get along home, Cindy, Cindy,
   Get along home, Cindy, Cindy,
   I'll marry you some time.

SOURWOOD MOUNTAIN

This is one of the most popular tunes among mountain musicians. Like most of the fiddle tunes, its origin is hidden in the mystery of time. The words are undoubtedly of American origin. This song, too, was sung by Aunt Jennie Wilson.

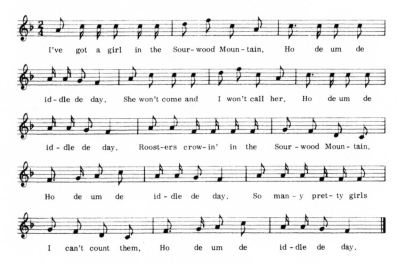

I've got a girl in the Sour-wood Moun-tain, Ho de um de id-dle de day. She won't come and I won't call her, Ho de um de id-dle de day. Roost-ers crow-in' in the Sour-wood Moun-tain, Ho de um de id-dle de day. So man-y pret-ty girls I can't count them, Ho de um de id-dle de day.

2 Big dogs bite and little ones bite you,
    Ho de um de iddle de day.
  Big girls court and little ones fight you,
    Ho de um de iddle de day.
  My true-love lives up in Letcher,
    Ho de um de iddle de day.
  She won't come and I won't fetch her,
    Ho de um de iddle de day.

3 I've got a girl at the head of the holler,
    Ho de um de iddle de day.
  She won't come and I won't foller,
    Ho de um de iddle de day.

180

Old man, old man, can I have your daughter,
   Ho de um de iddle de day.
To bake me bread and carry me water,
   Ho de um de iddle de day.

GROUNDHOG

The origin of this humorous song is unknown. One singer told me that it was "put together" in Calhoun County, but that is not likely. There are several versions of the tune, and some texts have more stanzas.

The groundhog, or woodchuck, is a well-known pest among West Virginia farmers. However, it was also often useful, for the meat was eaten by many people, and the hide was tanned to be used for shoe laces. In the process of tanning, the hide was placed in a stone jar or a cast-off churn and covered with wood ashes to remove the hair, which explains the line, "The hide's in the churn."

When the groundhog took refuge in a hollow log it could be twisted out with a forked stick. It was called a "whistlepig" because of the loud shrill whistle which it sometimes gave. This version was sung by Dewey Bourn, Braxton County.

Shoul-der up my axe, whis-tle up my dog, Shoul-der up my axe, whis-tle up my dog, Go - in' up the hol - ler to ketch a groun' - hog. Groun' - hog!

2 One in the rocks, and two in the log,
    One in the rocks, and two in the log,
    I heard one whistle and knowed it was a hog.
        Groun'hog!

3 Run here, Tom, with a ten-foot pole,
    Run here, Tom, with a ten-foot pole,
    Twist that groun'hog outen his hole.
        Groun'hog!

4 Took that pole and twisted him out,
   Took that pole and twisted him out,
   Good Lord-a-mighty, ain't a groun'hog stout!
   Groun'hog!

5 Took him home and tanned his hide,
   Took him home and tanned his hide,
   Made the best shoestrings I ever tried!
   Groun'hog!

6 Yander comes Bill with a snigger and a grin,
   Yander comes Bill with a snigger and a grin,
   Groun'hog grease all over his chin.
   Groun'hog!

7 Old Aunt Sal hoppin' with her cane,
   Old Aunt Sal hoppin' with her cane,
   Swore she'd have the whistlepig's brain.
   Groun'hog!

8 Old Aunt Sal skippin' through the hall,
   Old Aunt Sal skippin' through the hall,
   She had enough whistlepig to grease them all.
   Groun'hog!

9 The meat's in the kibberd, the hide's in the churn,
   The meat's in the kibberd, the hide's in the churn,
   If that ain't groun'hog, I'll be durned!
   Groun'hog!

A PAPER OF PINS

This is an action song. It is a dialogue between a girl and a boy, often dramatized for the entertainment of audiences at socials. It was sung by Ivy Lee Myers, of Gilmer County.

"I'll give to you a pa-per of pins, And that's the way our love be-gins, If you will mar-ry, mar-ry me, If you will mar-ry me."

2 "I'll not accept your paper of pins,
   If that's the way our love begins,
   And I'll not marry, marry you,
   And I'll not marry you."

3 "I'll give to you a dress of red,
   Stitched all around with golden thread,
   If you will marry, marry me,
   If you will marry me."

4 "I'll not accept your dress of red,
   If that's the way our love begins,
   And I'll not marry, marry you,
   And I'll not marry you."

5 "I'll give to you a dress of green,
   That you may look just like a queen,
   If you will marry, marry me,
   If you will marry me."

6 "I'll not accept your dress of green,
  If that's the way our love begins,
  And I'll not marry, marry you,
  And I'll not marry you."

7 "I'll give to you a little tray dog,
  To go with you when you walk abroad,
  If you will marry, marry me,
  If you will marry me."

8 "I'll not accept your little tray dog,
  If that's the way our love begins,
  And I'll not marry, marry you,
  And I'll not marry you."

9 "I'll give to you a coach and six,
  Six black horses black as pitch,
  If you will marry, marry me,
  If you will marry me."

10 "I'll not accept your coach and six,
   If that's the way our love begins,
   And I'll not marry, marry you,
   And I'll not marry you."

11 "I'll give to you the key to my heart,
   That we may marry and never part,
   If you will marry, marry me,
   If you will marry me."

12 "I'll not accept the key to your heart,
   If that's the way our love begins,
   And I'll not marry, marry you,
   And I'll not marry you."

13 "I'll give to you the key to my chest,
   That you may have money at your request,
   If you will marry, marry me,
   If you will marry me."

14 "I will accept the key to your chest,
   If that's the way our love begins,
   And I will marry, marry you,
   And I will marry you."

15 "O miss, I see that money is all,
And woman's love means nothing at all,
So I'll not marry, marry you,
And I'll not marry you."

PART FOUR

Choral Singing in the Mountains

Even before our pioneer ancestors built their churches in the wilderness, they often cleared out a patch of woods to make way for a meeting place where the itinerant minister could get the people together for a religious meeting. With all religions, singing is an important part of the worship service. There were very few hymn books; even if there had been books, many of the people could not read the songs. How, then, did the people learn to sing the hymns together?

The system of learning the old hymns was called "lining out" the song. The minister would have with him a book of hymns containing only the words, with an indication of the metrical pattern of the lines: long meter, short meter, or common meter, or if the meter did not fit any of these patterns, there would be numbers indicating the number of syllables in each line of verse. There might also be printed under the title of the song the name of a hymn tune that would be suitable for this particular hymn. The minister, or some capable leader in the congregation, would "line out" the song by singing the first line, and the congregation would repeat it. Then each line of the song would be learned in the same manner until the entire song became familiar. This was the way people learned to sing together at religious meetings in the early days, until a new way of teaching music was invented early in the nineteenth century.

This new approach was the "shape-note" method of writing music.

It was brought south from Pennsylvania by the German settlers who migrated into the Shenandoah Valley, where Harrisonburg, Virginia, became an early center for the printing of shape-note song books. Men who became familiar with the use of shape-notes began to go out to the rural communities to teach singing school by this method. Following the Civil War these men (whom we always called "singin' masters" when I was a boy) came over the Allegheny Mountains into the rural communities of what by then had become West Virginia.

The singing master would send word to a community that he would come there and teach a subscription singing school. This meant that all families that wished to participate would subscribe a small amount to pay the teacher, who would "board round" among these families during the period of ten days or two weeks while the singing school lasted. The people would purchase books from the singing master, so that soon all the people in the community, young and old, could read music and sing harmony with ease. Someone in the community would be selected to lead the singing, and one of the most important and popular activities of the community was the weekly "singing" held at one of the churches, where the entire evening was spent in singing the old hymns.

In the shape-note method of music, each note of the scale is shaped so that its position in the scale can be immediately determined by its shape:

Numeral names.	1,	2,	3,	4,	5,	6,	7,	8.
Pitch names.	C,	D,	E,	F,	G,	A,	B,	C.
Syllable names.	Do,	Re,	Mi,	Fa,	Sol,	La,	Ti,	Do.

Do is moveable, its position on the staff being determined by the key signature. In the key of C, *Do* is C; in the key of D, *Do* is D; in the key of A, *Do* is A, and so on.

The singing master always had a tuning fork to determine the correct pitch, but the community song leader rarely had any means of obtaining the correct pitch for a song, since country churches had no musical instruments until fairly late years. The leader developed "pitch-memory," and could usually determine the correct pitch from memory.

The "singing" at the church one night each week became a very important factor in the development of community life. It was where young people got to know one another, where many a match was made, where families intermingled and exchanged knowledge and ideas. When there was a death in the community, the emergency ring was given on the party line and the church bell was tolled, so that a large choir would assemble. Choirs sang at wakes also, and at public meetings.

Seven of the hymns which we have included in this book are written in shape-note music: "What Wondrous Love;" "Brethren, We Have Met to Worship;" "I will Arise and Go to Jesus;" "Rock of Ages;" "Amazing Grace;" "Jesus, Lover of My Soul;" and "The Church's One Foundation."

CHRIST WAS BORN IN BETHLEHEM

This old religious ballad in the five-tone scale is not well-known in West Virginia. I learned it from my Grandfather Gainer when I was a boy. He used to sit on his porch on a Sunday morning in summer and sing old favorites like this one.

Christ was born in Beth - le - hem, Christ was born in Beth - le - hem,

Christ was born in Beth - le - hem, And in the man - ger lay. And

in a man - ger lay, And in a man - ger lay.

Christ was born in Beth - le - hem and in the man - ger lay.

2 The Jews they crucified him, (3)
   They nailed him to the cross.

3 Joseph begged his body, (3)
   And laid it in the tomb.

4 The tomb it would not hold him, (3)
   He burst the bands of death.

5 Down came an angel, (3)
   And rolled the stone away.

6 Mary she came weeping, (3)
   Her blessed Lord to see.

7 Go tell your brethren, (3)
   He's risen from the dead.

THE PILGRIM OF SORROW

This is a good example of the kind of religious song that people learned by the "lining out" method, long before harmony came into use. Note the simplicity of the musical structure, with the first musical phrase being repeated, the only variation being in the chorus, which follows each stanza. Sung by Hobart Napier, of Logan County.

I __ am a poor pil-grim of sor - row, __ Cast out in this wide world to roam. __ My __ broth-ers and sis-ters won't own me. __ They say that I'm weak and I'm poor. __ But Je - sus, the Fa - ther al - might-y __ Has bade me to en - ter the door. __ Some - times I'm al - most driv - en, __ Till I know not where to roam, __ I've heard of a cit - y called heav - en, __ I've start-ed to make it my home. __

2 My mother has reached the bright glory,
   My father's still walking in sin.
   My brothers and sisters won't own me,
   Because I am trying to get in.
   Chorus:

192

3 When friends and relations forsake me,
And troubles roll round me so high,
I think of the kind words of Jesus,
Poor pilgrim I am always nigh.
Chorus:

4 Oh, soon I shall reach the bright glory,
Where mortals no more do complain,
The ship that will take me is coming,
The captain is calling my name.
Chorus:

THE WAYFARING PILGRIM

This religious song is sometimes called "The Wayfaring Stranger." It was sung more often as a solo than as a choral song, but like all of the old songs first learned by the "lining out" method, it took on something of the character of each singer who learned it and passed it on in tradition. No two folk singers ever sing the same song exactly alike, but one will add notes, holds, and vocal effects to the song. Indeed, the same singer may vary a song somewhat each time he sings it. Mr. J. T. Lockard, of Braxton County, was ninety-five years old when he sang this song for me.

I'm a poor way-far-ing pil-grim, While trav'l-ing through this world below. There'll be no sick-ness, toil, or dan-ger In that bright
land to which I go; I'm go-ing there to see my
fa-ther; I'm go-ing there no more to roam. I am
go-ing o-ver Jor-dan, I'm just go-ing o-ver home.

    2 I know dark clouds will gather round me,
       I know my road is rough and steep.
       But golden fields lie up before me,
       While a pilgrim I no more shall weep.
       I'm going there to see my mother,
       She said she'd meet me when I came.
       I am going over Jordan,
       I'm just going over home.

3 I want to sing salvation's story,
  In concert with the blood-washed men.
  I want to wear a crown of glory,
  When I get home to that good land.
  I'm going there to see my classmates,
  Who passed before me one by one.
  I am going over Jordan,
  I'm just going over home.

4 I'll soon be free from ev'ry trial,
  My body'll rest in the old churchyard.
  I'll drop the cross of self-denial,
  And enter into my reward.
  I'm going there to see my Saviour,
  Who shed His precious blood for me.
  I am going over Jordan,
  I'm just going over home.

WHEN I SET OUT FOR GLORY

The only person I ever heard sing this song was Aunt Mary Wilson. So far as I know, nothing is known of its origin. Aunt Mary sometimes "got happy and shouted" at meetings, singing this song as she moved gracefully from one side of the church to the other. It is in the mixolydian mode.

When I set out for glo - ry, I left this world be - hind, De -
ter-mined for a cit - y Is out of sight to find. Then be -

CHORUS

lieve on your Je - sus, be - lieve on your God, Be -

lieve on your Je - sus, And heav - en is your re - ward.

2 Some say I'd better tarry,
   Some say I am too young
   To prepare for dying,
   And that is all my song.
   (Chorus after each stanza)

3 Oh, do not be discouraged,
   For Jesus is your friend,
   And if you look for knowledge
   He will not refuse to lend.

4 And if you meet with trials
   And troubles on your way,
   Just cast your cares on Jesus,
   And don't forget to pray.

196

5 But now I am a soldier,
  My Captain's gone before,
  He gives me my orders,
  And tells me never to give o'er.

6 Guard on your heavenly armor
  Of hope, faith, and love,
  And when the war is over,
  We'll reign with Christ above.

7 Come all you poor backsliders,
  Come listen to my cry,
  It's all you poor backsliders
  Must shortly beg or die.

8 I do not ask for riches,
  Nor to be dressed so fine,
  The garment that he's given me,
  The sun it will outshine.

WHAT WONDROUS LOVE

We have printed this old song in shape notes, but it existed as part of the oral tradition long before the use of written music among mountain people. The method used then was "lining out." I learned it in the "Singin' School."

What won-drous love is this, O my soul, O my soul! What won-drous love is this, O my soul! What won-drous love is this, That caused the Lord of bliss, To bear the dread-ful curse For my soul, For my soul, To bear the dread-ful curse For my soul.

2 To God and to the Lamb,
   I will sing, I will sing.
   To God and to the Lamb,
   I will sing.
   To God and to the Lamb,
   And to the great I Am,
   While millions join the psalm,
   I will sing, I will sing,
   While millions join the psalm,
   I will sing.

BRETHREN, WE HAVE MET TO WORSHIP

The name of the tune is Holy Manna. *The numbers following the name of the tune indicate the metrical pattern of the lines. The first line has eight syllables, followed by a line of seven syllables. It uses the pentatonic scale. This song, too, was sung in the "Singin' School."*

Holy Manna. 8s. 7s.

2 Brethren, see poor sinners round you slumb'ring on the brink of woe;
Death is coming, hell is moving, can you bear to let them go?
See our fathers and our mothers, and our children sinking down;
D.C. Brethren, pray, and holy manna will be showered all around.

3 Sisters, will you join and help us? Moses' sister aided him;
  Will you help the trembling mourners who are struggling hard with
    sin?
  Tell them all about the Savior, tell them that He will be found;
  D.C. Sisters, pray, and holy manna will be showered all around.
    Amen.

I WILL ARISE AND GO TO JESUS

The name of the tune, also from the "Singin' School," is Arise. *The numbers after the name of the hymn tune indicate that the first line has eight syllables, the second has seven, the third has eight, the fourth has seven, the fifth has four, and the last line has seven. With written music, this indication of the metrical pattern of the line is unnecessary, but it was important for the selection of a tune for "lining out."*

Arise. 8.7.8.7.4.7.

2 Come, ye thirsty, come, and welcome, God's free bounty glorify;
True belief and true repentance, ev'ry grace that brings you nigh.
(Chorus after each stanza)

3 Come, ye weary, heavy-laden, lost and ruined by the fall;
If you tarry till you're better, you will never come at all.

4 Let not conscience make you linger, nor of fitness fondly dream;
All the fitness He requireth is to feel your need of Him. Amen.

ROCK OF AGES

This old hymn, taught in the singing schools in shape notes, became one of the favorites for wakes, funerals, and religious meetings.

Rock of A - ges, cleft for me, Let me hide my-self in Thee;

Let the wa - ter and the blood, From Thy wound-ed side which flowed.

Be of sin the dou - ble cure. Save from wrath and make me pure.

2 Could my tears forever flow, could my zeal no languor know,
These for sin could not atone; Thou must save, and Thou alone;
In my hand no price I bring, simply to Thy cross I cling.

3 While I draw this fleeting breath, when my eyes shall close in death,
When I rise to worlds unknown, and behold Thee on Thy throne,
Rock of Ages, cleft for me, let me hide myself in Thee.

AMAZING GRACE

No other old hymn has been more popular than "Amazing Grace." It passed into the stream of tradition and became known "by heart" to almost everyone in rural West Virginia, as in many other parts of America.

A - maz - ing grace how sweet the sound That saved a wretch like me! I once was lost, but now I'm found, Was blind but now I see.

2 'Twas grace that taught my heart to fear, and grace my fears relieved;
How precious did that grace appear, the hour I first believed.

3 Through many dangers, toils and snares, I have already come;
'Tis grace that brought me safe thus far, and grace will lead me home.

4 When we've been there ten thousand years, bright shining as the sun;
We've no less days to sing God's praise, than when we first begun.

MUST JESUS BEAR THE CROSS ALONE?

This song has been included in this volume because it has long been sung whenever country people gathered together for singing. Books were not needed to sing this song in harmony, for everyone knew it "by heart."

Must Je - sus bear the cross a - lone,_ And all the world go free?_

No, there's a cross for ev -'ry one._ And there's a cross for me._

2 The consecrated cross I'll bear, till death shall set me free,
   And then go home my crown to wear, for there's a crown for me.

3 Upon the crystal pavement, down at Jesus' pierced feet,
   Joyful, I'll cast my golden crown, and His dear name repeat.

4 O precious cross! O glorious crown! O resurrection day!
   Ye angels, from the stars come down, and bear my soul away.

JESUS, LOVER OF MY SOUL

We have included this beautiful hymn in shape notes, not because it is a folk song in the true sense of the term, but because it became known to all singers and was sung at most wakes, funerals, and religious gatherings. Martyn *is the name of the tune to which it is sung, and the metrical pattern has seven syllables doubled.*

Martyn 7s.D.

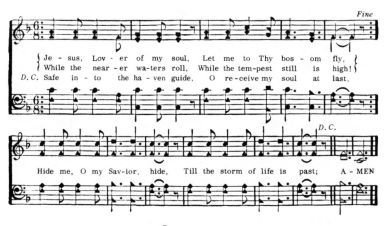

Je - sus, Lov - er of my soul, Let me to Thy bos - om fly,
While the near - er wa-ters roll, While the tem-pest still is high!
D.C. Safe in - to the ha - ven guide, O re-ceive my soul at last.

Hide me, O my Sav-ior, hide, Till the storm of life is past; A - MEN

THE CHURCH'S ONE FOUNDATION

This hymn is not a folk song, but it is included because so many people have requested it. Musically, it represents a great step away from the modal tunes of the old songs. This is not the kind of hymn that was "lined out."

The Church's one foun-da-tion Is Je-sus Christ her Lord;

She is His new cre-a-tion By wa-ter and the word:

From heav'n He came and sought her To be His ho-ly bride; With

His own blood He bought her, And for her life He died.

2 Elect from ev'ry nation, yet one o'er all the earth,
Her charter of salvation, one Lord, one faith, one birth;
One holy name she blesses, partakes one holy food,
And to one hope she presses, with ev'ry grace endued.

3 'Mid toil and tribulation, and tumult of her war,
She waits the consummation, of peace for evermore;
Till, with the vision glorious, her longing eyes are blest,
And the great church victorious shall be the church at rest.

4 Yet she on earth hath union with God the Three in One,
And mystic sweet communion with those whose rest is won:
O happy ones and holy! Lord, give us grace that we,
Like them the meek and lowly, on high may dwell with Thee. Amen.

PART FIVE

The Negro Contribution

The Negro contribution to American folk music is far greater than that made by any other ethnic group or race in America. The white people who came to America from foreign lands brought with them in their oral tradition their music, which they continued to preserve in family life. They had no need to develop new music in order to adapt to their new environment. On the other hand, the blacks, brought to America as slaves, came from various parts of Africa and did not have a common body of song or even a common language. Thrown together in their new environment under bondage, they had to develop a common body of song, for it is a fact that no body of people ever live together very long without expressing themselves in song as a group and as individuals.

From the new religious experience, which came as a result of the preaching of their white Christian captors, came the spirituals. The words came from passages from the Bible and from sermons on the sinfulness of the worldly life and the promise of a happy life in eternity. It is astonishing that there is a total lack of bitterness toward their captors in these deeply religious songs, but only love for God and fellow man. The music of the spirituals is chiefly African in its origin, and the spirituals in their origin are a spontaneous overflow of feeling and emotion in song. They are not solo songs, but are choral in structure. They require a leader and a chorus.

The spirituals were first made known to the world at large by a small group of singers who went out from Fisk University in 1871-72, calling themselves "The Jubilee Singers." The story of their triumphs and their hardships in a society which loved their singing but rejected them socially, is well related in a book by J.B.T. Marsh, *The Story of the Jubilee Singers.* This story should be known by every young American. I recommend also the book by John W. Work, *Negro Spirituals and Blues,* an excellent, objective study.

The relatively few blacks who came to West Virginia (there was little slavery in the State) worked mainly on the railroads and in the mines. They brought with them their traditional songs, which soon became known to the white people in the hills.

NOBODY KNOWS THE TROUBLE I SEE

It should be noted that in printing the songs in this book we have not used any dialectal pronunciations. Speech is not racial but is environmental, whether it is the speech of the white people of the mountains or that of the black people in the southern region. It would be impossible to print the speech of each singer exactly as it sounded when he sang. Although the six following spirituals represent contributions to our American folk music by black Americans, these songs have been sung just as much by white Americans through the years. Contributed by Mr. C. W. Wiley, Raleigh County.

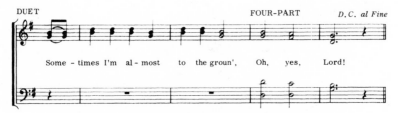

Sometimes I'm almost to the groun', Oh, yes, Lord!

2 Although you see me going 'long so, oh, yes, Lord!
  I have my troubles here below, oh, yes, Lord!

  Nobody knows the trouble I see, nobody knows my sorrow;
  Nobody knows the trouble I see, glory hallelujah!

3 What makes old Satan hate me so, oh, yes, Lord!
  'Cause he got me once and let me go, oh, yes, Lord!

  Nobody knows the trouble I see, nobody knows my sorrow;
  Nobody knows the trouble I see, glory hallelujah!

GO DOWN, MOSES

This well-known spiritual is based on **Exodus**. When sermons described the story of the Israelites under bondage in Egypt and how Moses led them to freedom, it was natural for the black slaves in America to liken their own plight to that of God's chosen people. It is a plea that they may flee from worldly troubles to be free in Christ. Contributed by Mr. C. W. Wiley.

Tell ole Phar-aoh, _____ Let my peo-ple go.

2 Thus saith the Lord, bold Moses said,
   If not, I'll smite your first-born dead.

3 O, 'twas a dark and dismal night,
   When Moses led the Israelites.

4 The Lord told Moses what to do,
   To lead the children of Israel through.

5 O come along Moses, you'll not get lost,
   Stretch out your rod and come across.

6 As Israel stood by the water side,
   At the command of God it did divide.

7 When they had reached the other shore,
   They sang the song of triumph o'er.

8 Pharaoh said he would go across,
   But Pharaoh and his host were lost.

9 O Moses the cloud shall clear the way,
   A fire by night, a shade by day.

10 You'll not get lost in the wilderness,
   With a lighted candle in your breast.

11 Jordan shall stand up like a wall,
   And the walls of Jericho shall fall.

12 Your foes shall not before you stand,
   And you'll possess fair Canaan's land.

13 'Twas just about in harvest-time,
   When Joshua led his host divine.

14 O let us all from bondage flee,
   And let us all in Christ be free.

15 We need not always weep and moan,
   And wear these slavery chains forlorn.

WADE IN THE WATER

I first heard this spiritual in 1958 when "Uncle" John Hunter, of Logan County, sang it for me. Because, like most of the spirituals, it requires a leader and a chorus, Mr. Hunter said he needed help to sing it. Members of his family and I all joined in to form the chorus while Mr. Hunter sang the part of the leader. He was ninety-three at the time, and he said it made him feel mighty good to sing.

Wade in the wa - ter, Wade in the wa - ter, chil - dren,

Wade in the wa - ter, God's a - going to trou - ble the wa - ter; O wa - ter.

LEADER

See that host all dressed in white, God's a - going to trou - ble the wa - ter;

Hum......................

The Lead-er looks like the Is-rael-ite, God's a-going to trou-ble the wa-ter.

Hum.....................

2 O see that band all dressed in red, God's a-going to trouble the water;
Looks like the band that Moses led, God's a-going to trouble the
water.
Wade in the water, wade in the water, children,
Wade in the water, God's a-going to trouble the water.

3 O look over yonder, what do I see? God's a-going to trouble the
water;
The Holy Ghost a-coming on me, God's a-going to trouble the water.
Wade in the water, wade in the water, children,
Wade in the water, God's a-going to trouble the water.

4 O if you don't believe I've been redeemed, God's a-going to trouble
the water;
Just follow me down to Jordan's stream, God's a-going to trouble the
water.
Wade in the water, wade in the water, children,
Wade in the water, God's a-going to trouble the water.

LORD, I WANT TO BE A CHRISTIAN

There is probably no spiritual as deeply religious as this one, a favorite with all Christian people, white or black. Note that there is neither fourth nor seventh in its musical structure. Contributed by Mr. C. W. Wiley.

2 Lord, I want to be more loving in-a my heart, in-a my heart,
Lord, I want to be more loving in-a my heart.
In-a my heart, in-a my heart, in-a my heart, in-a my heart,
Lord, I want to be more loving in-a my heart.

3 Lord, I want to be more holy in-a my heart, in-a my heart,
Lord, I want to be more holy in-a my heart.
In-a my heart, in-a my heart, in-a my heart, in-a my heart,
Lord, I want to be more holy in-a my heart.

4 I don't want to be like Judas in-a my heart, in-a my heart,
I don't want to be like Judas in-a my heart.
In-a my heart, in-a my heart, in-a my heart, in-a my heart,
I don't want to be like Judas in-a my heart.

5 Lord, I want to be like Jesus in-a my heart, in-a my heart,
Lord, I want to be like Jesus in-a my heart.
In-a my heart, in-a my heart, in-a my heart, in-a my heart,
Lord, I want to be like Jesus in-a my heart.

SWING LOW, SWEET CHARIOT

It is doubtful that there is any singer in America who cannot sing this beautiful old spiritual, with its joyous spirit of hope. It uses the pentatonic scale.

Swing low, sweet char - i - ot, ___ Com - ing for to car - ry me home. Swing low, sweet char - i - ot, ___ Com - ing for to car - ry me home. I looked o - ver Jor - don, and what did I see? ___ Com - ing for to car - ry me home. A band of an - gels

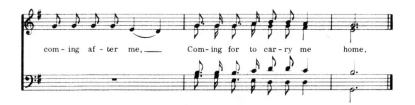

com - ing af - ter me, ____ Com- ing for to car - ry me home.

2 If you get there before I do,
Coming for to carry me home,
Tell all my friends I'm coming too,
Coming for to carry me home.

Swing low, sweet chariot,
Coming for to carry me home,
Swing low, sweet chariot,
Coming for to carry me home.

3 I'm sometimes up and sometimes down,
Coming for to carry me home,
But still my soul feels heavenward bound,
Coming for to carry me home.

Swing low, sweet chariot,
Coming for to carry me home,
Swing low, sweet chariot,
Coming for to carry me home.

IT'S ME, O LORD

Note again the musical structure of this song. If you sing the tune by the syllables of the scale—do, re, mi, fa, sol, la, ti, do—which syllables will not be used? Most of the spirituals use the pentatonic scale. If a seventh appears, it is often flatted. Contributed by Mr. C. W. Wiley.

It's me, it's me, O Lord, Stand-in' in the need of pray'r, It's me, it's me, O Lord, Stand-in' in the need of pray'r. Not my moth-er, not my fa-ther, but it's me, O Lord. Stand-in' in the need of pray'r. Not my moth-er, not my fa-ther, but it's

me,   O   Lord,   Stand-in'   in   the   need   of   pray'r.

BIBLIOGRAPHY

Child, Francis James. *The English and Scottish Popular Ballads*, 5 vols., Houghton Mifflin, 1882-1898. Republished in paperback edition, 5 vols. Dover Publications, Inc., 1965.

Cox, John Harrington. *Folk Songs Of the South*. Harvard University Press, 1925. Words only of songs collected in West Virginia.

Journal of American Folklore (Organ of the American Folklore Society). Boston, 1887 ————.

Sargent, Helen C. and Kittredge, G. L. *English and Scottish Popular Ballads*. (1 vol. selection from Child's full work.) Houghton Mifflin, 1904.

Sharp, Cecil J. *English Folk Songs From the Southern Appalachians*, ed. Maud Karpeles. 2 vols. Oxford University Press, 1932.

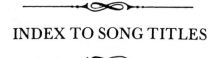

INDEX TO SONG TITLES

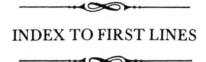

INDEX TO FIRST LINES